No **CHOICE** *but to* **CHOOSE**

Confronting the New Assault on Human
Agency and Achievement in Business

No **CHOICE**
but to **CHOOSE**

**Confronting the New Assault on Human
Agency and Achievement in Business**

Barry L. Linetsky

Linetsky, Barry

No Choice but to Choose: The New Assault on Human Agency and Achievement in Business / Barry Linetsky.

ISBN: 9798637211180
Independently Published by the author.

1. Free will. 2. Iconoclasm. 3. Thinking. 4. Creative Ability. 5. Mind/Body Dualism. 6. Materialism. 7. Scientific Method. 8. Induction and Deduction. 9. Reductionism. 10. Neuroeconomics. 11. Elliott Jaques. 12. Gregory Berns. 13. Sam Harris. 14. Michael Gazzaniga. 15. Edwin Locke. 16. Leonard Peikoff.

www.BarryLInetsky.com

DEDICATION

This book is dedicated to everyone who takes philosophy seriously as a foundational discipline for seeking and finding knowledge and truth and by doing so consciously recognizes its practical importance in guiding their thinking, choices, and actions, in all realms of living a productive and fulfilling life, in accordance with reality.

This book is thereby also dedicated with love and admiration to Marlaine Koehler and our two fabulous daughters, Corinna and Leanne.

And, with a nod and a wink, to my university professor, Antony G.N. Flew.

CONTENTS

PREFACE

The question may arise in the mind of a curious reader why a non-academic entrepreneurial businessman would take the time to write a detailed critical analysis and response to a popular business book that very few people will ever read.

That question crossed my mind as what started out as a project to write a short book review of Gregory Berns' *Iconoclast: A Neuroscientist Reveals How To Think Differently* (Harvard Business Press, 2008) continued to grow in length. My conclusion is that it really has very little to do with the book itself, but rather with the current state of irrationality in our culture, and how false claims to knowledge based on faulty philosophic premises are harmful to the effective functioning of business organizations and the lives of people who depend on their success to earn a living and support their families (which includes almost everybody in modern society). *Iconoclast* is just one recent example of this phenomenon on a subject to which I felt I had something to contribute.

We live in a society in which people are not disposed to think very critically about important issues that fundamentally affect their lives. It seems that a high percentage of people are actively committed to remaining ignorant about important scientific, moral, political, and economic issues. Many wrongly believe in multiple and subjective realities, reason and logic as an unnecessary burden and constraint, ethics as a subjective standard that one sets for oneself based on how one feels at any given moment, and politics as a valid and necessary tool for coercing others to pursue means and ends considered to be desirable for some at the expense of others. At the fringe are the nihilists or extreme skeptics who claim that some or none of these things are important, either because they don't matter existentially, or because they claim that we have no real direct contact with reality and hence no way to really know the truth about anything.

As mistaken as these people are in their philosophical outlook, they have their own fringe thinkers which they look upon for support and guidance in providing assurances that their world view of nihilism and skepticism is valid. They look to the intellectuals and leaders in society for the validation of their mistaken ideas and beliefs. Way out on the fringe, in my opinion, are scientists who claim to have proof of the impossible—of the absurd—of square circles and perpetual motion machines. Professors who write books asking you to think about the arguments they put forth to prove claims that thinking is an illusion fall into this category. It reminds me of the old philosophy joke in which the solipsist can't understand why there aren't more people who are just like him given how convincing the proof is! (A solipsist believes that only one's own mind is sure to exist and therefore cannot know that the world and other minds exist.)

Yet today leading celebrity neuroscientists and biologists are publishing books and rushing forward with statements and elaborate arguments claiming that the scientific evidence overwhelmingly supports the conclusion that human agency is a cognitive illusion; that we have no free will; that we have been duped by our own brains into believing that we are capable of making choices; that our inner experience of considering future goals and making choices about which goals to pursue and the best paths to choose are merely illusions caused by uncontrollable causal chemical and physiological reactions in our brains. Many such luminaries of popular best-selling books as appear to be active defenders and promulgators of this idea. We'll meet some of them in this book.

Our culture is a reflection of the choices made and actions taken based on the beliefs and values of the individuals that make up that culture. Those in leadership roles in our social institutions such as business, government, universities and churches are not immune from bad ideas, and yet have the most influence in spreading them. In doing so they thereby promote the proliferation of their harmful effects when those mistaken ideas are inevitably acted upon. These harmful ideas are like mind viruses—memes—and can be just as destructive to human health, happiness, and flourishing.

There is nothing inherent in the higher education or status of a person's role in society that correlates to a higher degree of rationality or objectivity in the sense that their beliefs conform to reality. The opposite may be true. Our boardrooms, executive suites, lecture halls, laboratories and legislatures are full of men and women that are part of, and reflect the ideas, beliefs, values and behaviours of our society. To the degree that irrational men and women pervade the leadership ranks of society, those irrational ideas are set loose in word and deed to permeate all aspects of society. False ideas inevitably lead to actions that conflict with reality and therefore fail in their intent and result in some degree of harm. This is especially true when others are made to conform through legislated coercion and orchestrated personal attacks. Leaders, by the inherent nature of their position and control of economic inputs and resources, are the key purveyors of the ideas that guide and affect everyone else.

Underlying every idea is a more fundamental framework of ideas – a philosophy. It is a truism that to the extent that something is wrong philosophically in the sense that it clashes with reality and reason, it's not going to work in practice. Unfortunately we live in an age where few people understand the need for philosophy and its role in guiding human action, so almost nobody takes ideas seriously anymore, not even those who need them the most, like scientists, or those who deal in them for a living like teachers, university professors, politicians, and business managers.

In part this is because philosophy as a discipline to guide thinking and action is abstract and difficult. A more fundamental reason is that the discipline and rigour it imposes on thinking and action is seen as an unnecessary burden in a culture that embraces instant gratification and an escape from personal responsibility. In addition, and ironically, those seeking answers in philosophy as a guide to successful human achievement are right to reject the irrationalism offered by most philosophers who have failed in their task to provide practical and proper human guidance. As a result, individuals have no way to properly and fundamentally assess the validity of their premises and conclusions, and whether or not their choices or actions can achieve the intended results within a framework of individual rights and freedoms. And yet people must think, must make choices, and must act towards ends. Their welfare and survival depend on it.

In this regard, entrepreneurs, investors, and business leaders may be the last of a diminishing breed. It is they, by organizing capital and resources and bearing the risks of production that create employment opportunities for hundreds of millions, who best understand the impact of good and bad ideas. Their economic survival and those of the people they employ directly and indirectly depend on their ability to put true and valid ideas into action, and to avoid bad and invalid ideas.

The greatest burden of responsibility falls to the leaders of our organizations and institutions by virtue of their ability to affect the lives of so many people. The majority of men and women undertake their work seriously and are conscientious in doing their best to manage complexity and organize and lead their employees to achieve positive beneficial results.

But managerial leaders too are products of our modern culture. Most lack any philosophic training to detect and reject the constant influx and influence of unsound and possibly destructive ideas. Instead they rely on their common sense and appeals to social consensus and authority as they absorb ideas emanating from our leading universities, think tanks, and politicians. When destructive or ill-conceived ideas are accepted by managers, they inevitably become woven into the fabric of their organizations and infused into corporate cultures through policies, procedures, training, and personnel development programs.

Too often these guiding policies and procedures attempt to codify a framework for desirable values and actions in the workplace that fundamentally clash with reality and the objective requirements of business to profitably produce goods and services that customers value.

In reading Gregory Berns' *Iconoclast* I was struck by what in my opinion is a thesis built on faulty science and logic, and more fundamentally, guided by a philosophical viewpoint that openly clashes with reality. One doesn't have to be a scientist to reach this conclusion. I found it distressing that given all that is wrong with the underlying premises and arguments put forth in the book, and the author's apparent lack of understanding of what is required by workers to be productive in society, that it met the standard of the world's leading business publisher, Harvard Business Press, and is being offered as the latest in scientific insight to enlighten and guide influential business leaders and students of business. What makes it ironic is that if Dr. Berns' is correct, there could be no such thing as business. I have tried to parse the book into its key supporting threads and to present the essence of Dr. Berns' argument and ideas in what I hope is a readable dissertation.

It is important for those in senior business leadership roles to make the time and expend the effort to think critically about the validity and implications of the theories and underlying premises emanating from the leading thinkers in our leading business schools. False and therefore harmful theories go unnoticed because we think it acceptable for executives to make critical decisions of long-term impact based on one-page summaries (or worse, 280-character sound bites that pass for enlightened business thinking) issued by subordinates. Unless they are identified and rejected, those false and destructive theories and fads begin to settle into business discussions as valid and unquestioned underlying truths that must be adhered to. Adopting business theories built on false premises that clash with reality and can't be fully integrated into the context of our existing knowledge will inevitably result in business failure and wealth destruction that results in real dismal consequences for real human beings. It is not hyperbole to say that in some cases the universal application of these crazy ideas would lead to the destruction of civilization!

Whether we like it or not, the commitment we choose to put forth to identify and pursue valid ideas also has a moral dimension that we cannot escape.

No Choice But To Choose

INTRODUCTION

> After we came out of the church, we stood talking for some time together of Bishop Berkeley's ingenious sophistry to prove the nonexistence of matter, and that every thing in the universe is merely ideal. I observed, that though we are satisfied his doctrine is not true, it is impossible to refute it. I never shall forget the alacrity with which Johnson answered, striking his foot with mighty force against a large stone, till he rebounded from it – "I refute it thus."

Boswell: Life of Johnson[i]

Tens of thousands of business books are sold each year to people aspiring to learn the principles of success discovered and acted upon by the truly great business leaders. Success means acting in accordance to reality to achieve our goals. Readers on the hard road to discovery are hoping authors can provide some insight into timely solutions to existing and emerging business problems that stand in the way of our aspirations and potential well-being. The greatest of the great thinkers in any field—the true innovators that are able *to do things contrary to accepted wisdom* are identified as *iconoclasts* by Emory University psychiatrist and professor Gregory Berns, MD, Ph.D.

In his Harvard Business School book *Iconoclast: A Neuroscientist Reveals How to Think Differently* (Harvard Business Press, 2008), Dr. Berns sets out

---

[i] http://www.samueljohnson.com/refutati.html

to demonstrate to the reader the "science" behind the thinking that makes iconoclasts so astoundingly creative and successful.

As a neuroscientist, Dr. Berns focuses on biological aspects of the brain and takes a natural science (positivist) approach to studying iconoclasts and how they differ in kind from non-iconoclasts. He does this to the exclusion of a more integrated qualitative and inductive approach to scientific knowledge required by the social sciences and the study of the behaviour of man.

I will argue that this is a major methodological mistake on the part of Dr. Berns and other scientists who do likewise. This positivist approach to studying human action leads him into a materialistic and deterministic world-view about iconoclasts and their ability to think differently that is inherently irrational and therefore unconvincing to any business manager or executive that knows from first-hand experience that they and their workers are capable of rational thought, goal directed action, and personal accountability. For this reason and many others, the book Dr. Berns has penned is of no use whatsoever to its intended audience. It is harmful to the capabilities of managers to the extent that they may accept as valid many of Dr. Berns' underlying premises and stated conclusions, and to the extent to which they formulate or allow policies and practices based on such premises to infiltrate into the management system used to create value for customers, employees, shareholders, and other interested constituent groups.

The major shortcoming of *Iconoclast* is Dr. Berns' inclination to advance materialistic biological and neurological arguments as a substitute for and to the exclusion of the phenomenon of human thought, choice and action. Thinking requires identifying arguments, weighing evidence, and drawing conclusions. It is when these attributes are absent that thinking is absent, as is the case with computer processing. Computers do not think. They follow instructions. They proceed along a preprogrammed path. Their "thinking" is the codification of the thinking that has been done by humans with that capability.

At the root of thinking is the ability to identify facts, weigh evidence, and draw conclusions that can be acted upon to achieve values. Thinking, by definition, requires free will to the extent that we can control aspects of our cognitive facilities. To propose a theory of human cognitive processes that amounts to *deterministic* thinking, as Dr. Berns does, is self-contradictory and self-refuting.

For example, it seems absurd to put forward a theory to be taken seriously that would entail that the artists, animators, and directors who worked for Walt Disney had no capability to think, make choices, and influence their actions in imagining, designing, building, operating, marketing, and improving animated films, film-making technology, or Disneyland's ambiance and attractions. It is equally absurd to put forward that thousands of individuals acted as mere physical and chemical causal agents in the coordinated actions of designing, manufacturing, and assembling rocket parts and components to land a man on the moon and return him home safely. It seems obvious to us that these events are made possible by millions of freely made choices involving judgments taken in addressing and solving millions of problems, small and large, all along the economic and material supply chain and in doing the work itself. The end result of the creative-thinking process is not pre-determined and causally inevitable. It requires the effort of purposeful and focused thought and action. It requires human agency.

The idea of deterministic thinking is an ungrounded imaginary construct. It is science-fiction. It is also an incredulous claim because deterministic thinking entails that in all of Dr. Berns' research, preparing lectures and teaching, and in the writing of his book, he was unable and incapable of making choices that could have been otherwise. The claim isn't that choices are causal. Of course they are. We can't act in ways beyond the nature of our abilities. The claim by those who deny free will is that all human thought and action is at root causally determined by factors beyond our volitional control and are therefore inevitable and unavoidable.

Nonetheless, as we shall see, Dr. Berns stakes his thesis on this self-contradictory and self-refuting notion of "thinkingless" thinking, and as one might expect, delivers little of substance or interest to entrepreneurs or managers seeking a better understanding of the principles or patterns of thinking common to the people he identifies as iconoclasts. Nor is he able to provide any meaningful guidance to readers based on the neuroscientific study of actual iconoclasts to help readers in their desire for self-improvement and the achievement of greater personal success, elevated self-esteem, enhanced happiness, or improved business results.

In the end, the author of *Iconoclast* fails to instruct the interested reader on "how to think differently," even though that is the marketing claim on the book jacket. Worse, he claims that it is impossible for any non-iconoclast to think differently because people have almost no volitional control over *what* they think (content) or *how* they go about thinking (method).

These assertions or claims as scientific truths by Dr. Berns create a mind-numbing paradox. It is self-evident through introspective discovery and sharing of such experiences (though perhaps inexpedient for Dr. Berns' biological determinism) that people are able to initiate or suppress mental focus, think, and make non-predetermined and non-preordained choices to guide their actions. If it were otherwise, there could be no work, no business, no industry, and no civilization. More fundamentally, if it is true that free will is an illusion, there could be no *human* life whatsoever. Following Dr. Samuel Johnson with regards to the doctrine of determinism as it pertains to human thought and action, we can kick the rubber tires of our factory-built automobile in the showroom and repeat his famous immortal words: "I refute it *thus*."

In general, I will try to demonstrate that this ostensive action of kicking the tires of reality is enough for any rational and sane person to accept with complete confidence and assurance that it is human thinking and action that is the motor of the world. Leaders in all fields, and especially business executives and managers, must understand the issues at stake and take positive action to stem off the renewed assault on human freedom, achievement and responsibility. Our ability to lead prosperous, productive, meaningful, and successful lives depends on it.

The alternative lies in a new dark-ages of misery and poverty where life would be, in the immortal words of Thomas Hobbes, "solitary, poor, nasty, brutish, and short." Such an end is neither inevitable nor likely.

Dr. Berns' thesis is contradictory and nonsensical, which makes trying to explain it difficult. In the first part of this book I will introduce Dr. Berns' concepts to try to explain his thesis about iconoclasts, and point out some of the major implications and shortcomings of the world-view he and many others hold to be true and are intent on trying to win you over to their point-of-view through the assembly of carefully constructed arguments. The only thing we can compare his concepts and ideas to are other concepts and ideas and hold them up to the light of rational and valid methodological principles he claims as a scientist to adhere to. After introducing the reader to Dr. Berns arguments and evidence, we will turn to a more detailed assessment of the general thesis of free will, determinism, and a valid scientific methodology for studying human behavior.

Chapter 1

DEFINING THE ICONOCLAST

We begin by understanding who or what an iconoclast is so we can identify one when we come across him or her.

Dr. Berns begins his book with a definition of what he takes to be an iconoclast, stating that he will "operationalize the definition of an iconoclast as a person who does something that others say can't be done" (Berns, *Iconoclast*: 6). At first glance this seems to conform to our notions of an iconoclast as a great inventor or discoverer, as a person whose achievement changes the world. People like Galileo, Newton, Edison, Disney, Gates, Jobs, Branson and Musk come to mind. But this definition, when scrutinized as a scientific operational definition, is peculiar for a number of reasons.

For one thing, it is not based on what the iconoclast *does*, but on what "others" *think* about what another person does. The differentiating characteristic in this definition is not the person's intellectual, artistic, cultural or productive achievement, be it in reshaping society, or contribution to humankind, or in the heroic and courageous effort required to achieve the ends sought. The essential element that differentiates an iconoclast from others in Dr. Berns' definition is the *belief or opinion held by others* as to whether *what the person did could in fact be done*.

Let us consider this further to increase our understanding of Dr. Berns' definition using a hypothetical but realistic example, and let's leave aside for now that "others" is not defined, and not operationalized.

Imagine that "others" do not believe it is possible for a person to run a mile in under four minutes and then somebody breaks the four-minute barrier, as Roger Bannister did in 1954. By Dr. Berns' definition, that person is an iconoclast. Roger Bannister did something that others said couldn't be done.

But if "others" *do* believe that at some point in time someone (or a particular person, e.g., Bannister) will come along and run a mile in under four minutes, and a person does break the four-minute mile barrier (or that particular person), then that person is *not* an iconoclast. While it is the same action by the same person—running a mile in under four minutes—it is the categorization *by others* that determines iconoclast status, according to Dr. Berns.

Thus, by Dr. Berns' definition, it is not primarily the *doing* and the ensuing result that defines who is to be considered an iconoclast, but rather the *opinion of others* about the possibility of the doing. For Dr. Berns, doing something, such as accomplishing an extraordinary achievement, is a necessary but not sufficient condition to establish an individual as an iconoclast.

Dr. Berns' operational definition requires that "others" determine who are and are not iconoclasts based rightly or wrongly on their opinions, however formed.

As to *who* these skeptical "others" are that will define eligibility for iconoclast status, Dr. Berns provides no details or opinion. Does it refer to everybody, or to sub-groups? What if there is a situation where there are two camps in which some "others" think a man can run a four-minute mile and some think he can't? Dr. Berns' operational definition doesn't say whether the runner can be an iconoclast to some but not to others—whether he can simultaneously both be and not be an iconoclast as it pertains to running a mile in under four minutes (or any other achievement), but he implies and infers that consistent with Aristotle's law of excluded middle, a person either is or isn't, and can't simultaneously reside in both categories. Surely logic must play a role in the scientific method and the operationalizing of definitions.

These nagging questions demonstrate that Dr. Berns' operational definition as stated is not good enough. In fact, it is non-objective and thus inadequate to serve as a valid definition. As an operational definition, it doesn't allow the independent observer to identify when the condition of "iconoclast" has been met. This isn't really a serious issue for Dr. Berns because, as we will see, he doesn't pay much heed to his own definition. He begins with this operationalized definition as a pretense to the *form* of conventional scientific method, and not its actual practice. We will discover that what he *really* believes is that iconoclasts can be identified by their unique biological/neurological traits, regardless of the opinions of "others." We must conclude that Dr. Berns' operational definition fails, and therefore any arguments he attempts to build upon it will lack a valid conceptual and logical foundation, and thus are likely to be erroneous and non-scientific.

Defining an iconoclast this way based on non-essential characteristics of the concept (viz., the opinion of others) is akin to the way a painting gains the status of Masterpiece. In the art world, it is not so much the work of the artist that results in the 'masterpiece' label being attached. Rather, the label comes to be applied based on the opinions of influential curators, collectors, intellectuals, and other persons of influence in the art community (see Tom Wolfe, *The Painted Word*, 1975).

Let's look at another example, this time from the world of art, that Dr. Berns provides, to reinforce that the standard of identification of iconoclasts is, as with paintings, based on the opinion of others and not any objective facts about the achievement of the designated iconoclast. This will further reinforce that his operational definition is both inadequate and problematic in setting a sound foundation for what will follow.

Dr. Berns informs us that both Picasso and Van Gogh were iconoclasts, but only Picasso was a successful one, "at least during his lifetime" (Berns, *Iconoclast*: 130). That Van Gogh was not an iconoclast during his lifetime, or was an unsuccessful iconoclast, and either became an iconoclast or a successful iconoclast at some later point after his death, is asserted as a fact based solely on Van Gogh's rising posthumous fame and consumer interest in his work. Because his paintings haven't changed with the passing of time, the change in iconoclast status in Dr. Berns' eyes can't be attributed to any objective facts of the body of work itself. What can change over time is the opinion of others about the significance or value of the work, which can be greatly affected by marketing and other awareness-raising activities and events, including the argument from authority in assessing which works of art we are to accept as "great" or masterpieces.

When we consider Van Gogh, he seems to stand outside of the operational definition (what did Van Gogh do that others said could not be done?). Yet Dr. Berns says he meets the definition. Unfortunately the reader is left to wonder how or why it is that a person's rising or declining popularity over time is a criterion for awarding or rescinding iconoclast status; or who it is, if it is not our own personal judgment in each particular case, that decides whether and when the criteria has been met (the opinion of "others") to anoint a designate with iconoclast status. That Dr. Berns does not adhere to his own operational definition (which is an important means by which scientists strive to ensure methodological objectivity) should serve as a warning to the attentive reader to be wary of Dr. Berns' professed "scientific" approach and methodology to reaching valid and instructive scientific conclusions.

Consider another example that indicates that Dr. Berns' operational definition of iconoclast is problematic due to its subjectivity and arbitrariness. If someone like Van Gogh can become an iconoclast *after* his death, then why couldn't somebody be considered iconoclastic at one point in time but not at a later date?

Suppose hypothetically that in 1966 when comedian and movie star Jerry Lewis began his telethon to find a cure for Muscular Dystrophy (MD), the general opinion of "others" was that a cure for MD would *never* be found. And suppose in

5

1967 some brilliant or lucky scientist discovered a cure. By Dr. Berns' definition, the scientist that made the discovery would be an iconoclast by the fact of achieving something that "others" said could not be done.

Now let's go back to the situation in which a cure for MD hasn't yet been found. Suppose *today* the general consensus is that because of the rapid advances in biology, chemistry, genetics and medicine, one day a cure *will* be found, and sure enough, next year that same scientist, now in her late 60s, discovers that cure. That scientist would not be an iconoclast using Dr. Berns' definition, because there was a belief by "others" that a cure would be found. Or what if she was considered an iconoclast in 1967 when she discovered a cure, but fifty years later the consensus is that people in 1967 should have known that a cure *would be* found *some day*, so in fact she wasn't really an iconoclast – that the 1967 "others" were wrong. If Van Gogh can be granted iconoclast status after his death, I suppose by the same logic it's only appropriate that people can likewise have their status as iconoclast revoked at a later time. After all, peoples' opinions change, and different people in different times and places have different and conflicting opinions.

Because no operational definition of "others" is provided, we have no way of knowing or discovering who they are and by what method or standard they form their opinions. This is the case even though, according to Dr. Berns, it is they who decide something as important to Dr. Berns as which individuals will be elevated to the lofty and noble status of iconoclast – a category of people that he deems to be worthy of scientific study.

The failure by Dr. Berns to clearly define the means by which to identify an iconoclast for the purposes of his scientific study is extremely problematic with respect to the credibility of his scientific thesis and any conclusions he derives therefrom. When he talks about iconoclasts as a category of individuals, it is unclear to the reader who is being talked about as members of that category and what qualifies them for inclusion. Without a valid operational definition, it appears that the identification of an iconoclast is determined by the opinion of only one person, Dr. Berns himself, and that reference to an operational definition is only a pretense towards the *form* of scientific validity.

Chapter 2

CASTING OFF THE DEFINITIONAL CONSTRAINTS

Dr. Berns defines an iconoclast as "a person who does something that others say can't be done." Given the turbulent waters into which Dr. Berns launches his vessel, it isn't long before he finds that he needs to cast off that definitional anchor to help keep his ship afloat. He never formally rejects his original operational definition. Rather, he brings into consideration examples of iconoclasts that don't meet his definition, thereby signaling his intention to abandon it. This shouldn't be surprising given how imprecise it is as a definition (and thus how vague and useless it is as a scientific operationalized concept).

Dr. Berns fails to begin with a valid definition formulated from the essence of the characteristics that distinguish people who are 'iconoclasts' from those who are not. By identifying non-essential or even irrelevant attributes as the differentiating characteristics of iconoclasts, his argument based on his definition can't help but float free from the essential objective facts that form a valid concept and ties it to reality.

By failing to identify the essential characteristics of the concept *iconoclast*, he leaves the reader with the sense that something is wrong, or incomplete, even if the reader can't identify exactly what it is. There is a sense that the definition doesn't integrate with our general concept of what an iconoclast is, or with the attributes and characteristics that make an iconoclast different

9

from a non-iconoclast. It's okay for scientists and others to demonstrate that what we know is incorrect, or imprecise, or inadequate, or that new facts of nature or behavioural principles in the social sciences give us cause to question our perspectives on specific issues. But the onus of proof lies with those who propose new knowledge, and they must bear the burden for providing it. The rest of us are wise to proportion our belief to the evidence—*all* of the evidence relevant to a particular context.

Had Dr. Berns started his attempt to define an iconoclast where most of us begin, with the dictionary, he would have found that the *Oxford English Dictionary* definition for iconoclast makes reference to "one who assails cherished beliefs or venerated institutions on the ground that they are erroneous or pernicious." Using this as a starting point, if we want to add to the concept the condition of success in reshaping human thought and the course of human events, we can say that "an iconoclast is a person who discovers a better way of doing something that significantly reshapes the world or changes the way people think about the world." This definition captures the essence of iconoclast as a concept, where the *genus* is human being, and the *differentia* is a discovery or action that significantly changes the world. Other synonyms may include innovators, paradigm-shifters, or prime movers. To operationalize this, we would have to provide more precision to the word "significantly." But for general usage this isn't required.

While a proper definition identifies the essence of a valid concept, all of the other attributes of the referent still exist and are important but are excluded from the definition (but not the concept) because they are not part of its uniquely distinguishing characteristics. If unique and specific differentiating characteristics cannot be identified, then the concept is likely invalid (i.e., cannot be tied back directly to reality).

Given the OED definition of iconoclast above (which is a definition for general usage and not an operational definition), the following may all be true about iconoclasts, but are non-essential attributes, i.e., are not characteristics or attributes that make the concept unique. Iconoclasts may be philosophers, scientists, artists, entrepreneurs, athletes, etc. They may be male or female, young or old. They may come upon their discoveries by hard work or serendipity. Some may have had their discovery immediately acknowledged and accepted, and others may have had to fight against traditional thinking or existing vested interests to prove the validity of their viewpoint. Sometimes this will happen during their lifetime, and in other cases it may take centuries to validate their ideas. In some cases, the ideas of an iconoclast may be deemed valuable, and in others pernicious. Other people who are contemporaries of the iconoclast may have known about their work prior to its completion or proven success and have passed judgment on the probability of success, while still others may have learned about it only after the fact. Some may conclude that what the iconoclast has set out to do cannot be done (perhaps they themselves have tried and failed), while others may not be so skeptical, acknowledging that someday someone will come along and discover or invent a solution.

When one considers how illuminating the dictionary definition is, along with the solemn importance of the purpose of clear operational definitions when doing research to ensure the objectivity of one's methods and conclusions, it is peculiar that as a scientist Dr. Berns operational definition and concept of iconoclast so widely misses the mark.

As a general rule of thumb, I'm always skeptical of anyone who ignores accepted definitions of concepts unless they can demonstrate why the existing formulation of the concept is remiss, and why the newly provided formulation is an improvement, and not just self-serving.

Dr. Berns asserts his definition without any explanation or justification as to why it differs so radically from, or why we should accept it, over the accepted dictionary definition; and he offers up an operational definition that fails the test of *validity* (does it measure what it is supposed to measure?) and *reliability* (are the results the same when done by different people or by one person at different times?).

Dr. Berns discusses many people he takes to be iconoclasts in his book, both well-known and relatively unknown to the general public. These stories make for interesting reading. When we think of iconoclasts we think of people like Aristotle, Galileo, Kepler, Mozart, Newton, Michelangelo, Darwin, Jefferson, Franklin, Edison, Einstein, etc. We think of intellectuals, inventors, creators, entrepreneurs, politicians and scientists. We know their names and not those of their contemporaries precisely because they are iconoclasts. But there is nothing about Berns' operational definition that limits iconoclasts to people of this stature.

Had he adopted the OED definition he could have at least pointed to people who assail cherished beliefs or venerated institutions on the ground that such beliefs or institutions are erroneous or pernicious. Instead he chose to make "doing something that others say can't be done" his sole defining characteristic. But because this is non-essential to what an iconoclast is as a distinct concept differentiated from other concepts, it fails to provide proper guidance in the identification of iconoclasts and leaves the field wide-open.

Consider that as defined by Dr. Berns, it is possible that almost everybody was, is, or will be an iconoclast, in some manner or form. For example: none of the boy's teachers thought he could pass the college admission tests, but he did; none of the medical first responders thought the pilot could survive the plane crash, but he did; it was the generally accepted wisdom among players and coaches around the world that the team could not play at the level required to qualify to compete in the world championships, but they did; none of her family, friends, and colleagues thought she could learn enough Spanish in eight months to get a job in Mexico, but she did; nobody thought that he could ever become President of the United States, but he did. Or how about: because of his reputation for partying, nobody thought he could ever give up his rock & roll lifestyle to settle down and get married, but he did; because he smoked two packs of cigarettes per day, nobody thought he could give up smoking, but he did; because of her fear of heights and of flying, none of her family and friends thought she could get up the courage to go sky-diving, but she did, etc.

I may be accused of trivializing Dr. Berns intention, if not his words, but I would cite some of his own examples as a counter argument to such an accusation. Dr. Berns identifies the three women in the popular American band The Dixie Chicks as iconoclasts for the sole reason that as successful country music singers they took a personal stance against the U.S. war in Iraq: "The Chicks became iconoclasts when they took a stance against the dogma that said 'country music – unflagging patriotism" writes Dr. Berns (*Iconoclast*: 66). This is enough to make the Dixie Chicks iconoclasts and worthy of being included in Dr. Berns' studies.

This act of taking a stance in the face of opposition, if that is indeed the sufficient condition to include The Dixie Chicks in the set of iconoclasts, is not that uncommon. Politicians, educators, CEOs, clergy, media celebrities, husbands, wives, and children do it every day. Certainly, nobody would have said that these three female performers were incapable of taking a public stance against an unpopular war for which they would experience opposing viewpoints and have to defend themselves. This standard of taking a stance against a cliché dogma is a long way from the OED definition or common usage of the concept *iconoclast* and renders the threshold Dr. Berns sets to be an iconoclast extremely low. By this standard, perhaps the qualifications are so low that the spectre is raised as to whether there is any value in identifying and discussing iconoclasts as a special category of person worthy of distinct designation in the first place!

If being an iconoclast only requires that one stand up against a stereotypical dogma such as country music equals unflagging patriotism, or perhaps that punk and heavy metal bands can't sing songs about peace, love and understanding, then certainly anybody can by this means *choose* to be an iconoclast – with one important provision: that one accepts that people are agents capable of freely making such a choice. And there's the rub.

No Choice But To Choose

Chapter 3

YOU EITHER HAVE AN ICONOCLAST BRAIN OR YOU DON'T

Starting with his operational definition that an iconoclast is a person who does something that others say can't be done, Dr. Berns informs us that the ability of the iconoclast to do this "something" entails that "the iconoclast's brain is different" (Berns, *Iconoclast*: 6). Note that he doesn't say that the iconoclast uses his brain differently, or operates by a different set of principles, or methodology, or follows a different code of values, or has specific defining personality characteristics that we can learn from and adopt to improve our own life should we choose to do so. He doesn't offer "The 7 Highly Effective Habits of Iconoclasts" that we may learn from and mimic through the techniques of neurallinguistic programming (NLP), for example.

He doesn't posit that the iconoclast works harder or is more dedicated to thinking deeply about problems and their possible solutions or has a brain with the capability of operating at a higher cognitive level and with more insight into the nature of things than the average person. Nor does he say that it remains a mystery as to why some people are able to attain iconoclast stature and others are not, or that it amounts to education, determination, and luck.

Rather, Dr. Berns says that the brain of an iconoclast is different from a non-iconoclast in three respects, pertaining to *perception*, *fear response*, and *social intelligence*.

That's quite a bold and controversial claim to make—that iconoclasts are born with brains that are different, brains that cause them to be iconoclasts. It is a claim for which we should expect Dr. Berns to provide a preponderance of convincing evidence based on the study of iconoclasts. However, one soon comes to realize that no empirical evidence is offered or forthcoming in the book to demonstrate that genetics and environmental causes (i.e., nature) are the sole determinant of man's thinking and acting. Rather, Dr. Berns hopes to make his case through formal logical deduction and inference from a reductionist premise that amounts to the unsupported assertion that people lack free will.[1]

Implicit but unstated by Dr. Berns is that those "others" who are not iconoclasts have an uncanny and perhaps unerring ability to identify those who are the iconoclasts with different brains. They are able to do this by recognizing that iconoclasts have done something that the "others" said could not be done.

---

[1] For an opposite perspective supporting the overwhelming influence of nurture upon nature, see David Shenk, "Is There A Genius In All of Us?", BBC News Magazine, http://www.bbc.co.uk/news/magazine-12140064, January 12, 2011.

Chapter 4

DROWNING IN A WHIRLPOOL OF CIRCULAR THINKING

After establishing his basic premise that iconoclasts are people who do things that others say can't be done because they have brains that are different in kind from those others, Dr. Berns spends most of the book trying to provide support for this claim. Because he has not undertaken an inductive approach to studying iconoclasts, be it through magnetic resonance imaging of their brains or biographical studies, he has little direct empirical evidence to present. Instead he relies on a theoretical approach based on isolated laboratory research findings scattered over a period of more than 50 years. Dr. Berns believes that this adds up to a preponderance of evidence in support of his claim that iconoclasts have different brains, i.e., brains that are different in kind from the brains of non-iconoclasts.

Apart from the anecdotal stories and selective research results cited to support the hypothesis that iconoclasts possess three key traits (perceiving things differently, managing their fears, effectively selling their ideas), the primary reason his main argument is unconvincing is that it is circular, as follows:

Premise 1: Only those who do things others say can't be done are iconoclasts.

Premise 2: The brains of iconoclasts are different from the brains of non-iconoclasts.

Premise 3: Only those born with iconoclastic brains can be iconoclasts.

Conclusion: Therefore, only iconoclasts can do things others say can't be done.

What makes this an example of the fallacy of circular reasoning or "begging the question" is that the conclusion is essentially the same as Premise 1, which is Dr. Berns' operational definition of an iconoclast. To be convincing, Dr. Berns must forgo Premise 1, and prove the validity of Premise 2 and Premise 3 to derive the conclusion that only iconoclasts can do things that others say can't be done. As previously noted above, the definition of an iconoclast Dr. Berns provides is primarily dependent not on the achievement of the person deemed to be an iconoclast, but on the opinion of others as to whether or not something can be done. From the point of view of others, the accomplishments of the iconoclast are not intrinsic to any biological or neurological facts about those who are able to achieve results that others say can't be done. Seen this way, the attempt to travel this road for which Dr. Berns has set for himself is nothing less than a Quixotic quest.

Not only is the logic of Dr. Berns' main argument faulty, but just as important, his argument fails on scientific grounds because he does not provide sufficient evidence that there is such a thing as an iconoclastic brain that really exists (as distinct from the brain of a person identified as an iconoclast). He also fails to demonstrate that having a different *brain* in kind, rather than possessing other non-biological and non-neurological factors (such as the possession of an identifiable set of traits, skills, beliefs, values, dispositions, etc.), is the primary driver of doing something that others say can't be done.

Similarly, he fails to provide sufficient evidence to substantiate his deterministic "theory" of iconoclastic thinking as proposed in Premise 3 (only those born with iconoclastic brains can be iconoclasts). To weigh evidence or test a theory requires the freedom and ability to think. To think without human agency is a contradiction in terms, and invalidates the concept *thinking*. In fact, as we shall see, his materialist foundation for determinism (or psychological determinism) precludes him from providing any evidence at all that could remotely be considered a testable theory.

Chapter 5

THE ILLUSION OF THINKING?

As one begins to progress through *Iconoclast*, it becomes clear that Dr. Berns has an unusual way of presenting his argument, leading the reader to the frustrating conclusion that the veracity of his narrative cannot be trusted. Dr. Berns continuously makes assertions as foundational stepping-stones in building his case, and then abandons them while holding on to the conclusions he has put forth based on those earlier foundations. Dr. Berns' finds himself forced to slide amongst incompatible and contradictory positions as he tries to maintain some semblance of a reasoned argument for which there is no underlying and supporting logical foundation.

For example, Dr. Berns makes a big deal about the fact that iconoclasts *literally* see things differently:

> the first rule of iconoclasm: *he sees differently than other people*. Literally. (Berns, *Iconoclast*: 15. Italics in original).

What does the inclusion of "literally" mean? It means that at the sensory level, iconoclasts see things that non-iconoclasts do not see. But because he has no evidence to support this fantastic proposition, he later retracts it. He then proposes that it's not that iconoclasts literally see things differently, it's that they *perceive* them differently:

> The iconoclast doesn't literally see things differently than other people. More precisely, he

perceives things differently. (Berns, *Iconoclast*: 25. Italics in original).

Of course, this raises the question as to why he would make what he knows and admits is a false claim about the sight of iconoclasts in the first place.

Dr. Berns then also retracts the later assertion that iconoclasts *perceive* things differently! He asserts that what is different about iconoclasts is *not* how things are *perceived*, but how they *categorize* what they perceive:

> Although the spatial location of what we see may be important, most of what iconoclasts do differently from other people lies in how they categorize what they see. (Berns, *Iconoclast*: 28-29).

Is the ability to categorize differently an active methodological process of volitional thinking by iconoclasts that can be learned and taught to others? Apparently, it is not. Why not? Dr. Berns says that the *brains* of non-iconoclasts resist the process of the *mind* asserting itself to form new concepts. "By forcing the visual system to see things in different ways, you can increase the odds of new insights. It sounds remarkably simple. But it is not quite that easy... [T]he brain frequently resists exactly these types of new experiences because they cost energy to process" (Berns, *Iconoclast*: 34).

This introduction by Dr. Berns of a brain/mind dualism leads us deeper into the problem of free will and determinism and the notion that iconoclasts possess some semblance of free will. For Dr. Berns the brain frequently resists things it is forced by the mind to do. If a person could *learn* how to think in the manner of an iconoclast, then that person would have the ability to exert control over their brain—to think—which would make them an iconoclast. This, asserts Dr. Berns, is one of the differences in brains that is a distinguishing characteristic of the iconoclast. Those not born with an iconoclast brain can't think like an iconoclast. For Dr. Berns, biological destiny trumps volition.

A key to making sense of Dr. Berns' thesis is to understand his belief that non-iconoclasts lack the capacity for volitional consciousness (i.e., the ability to focus their mind to guide their conceptual thinking). His contention is that iconoclasts have some additional genetic disposition that gives them the mysterious ability to manipulate their mental faculty to categorize information in ways different from everybody else. The source of this difference is that they are born with a brain that is different in kind (as distinct from their ability to use their brains differently).

Dr. Berns appears at times to speak as if man has free will and can exert control over his consciousness, but a careful reading shows that this is not the case. Consider that Dr. Berns appears to grant that people can look at the same visual stimuli and interpret it differently. He writes that "Whether one person sees ugliness or beauty in asymmetry is entirely a result of categorization" (Berns, *Iconoclast*: 29). But Dr. Berns holds that categorization is, for the most part, beyond man's volitional control and requires no mental effort – that the brain *automatically* forms concepts and makes judgments from percepts and sensations. He goes on to say that the way we view the world isn't fixed because "the networks that govern both perception and imagination can be reprogrammed. The frontal cortex...can reconfigure neural networks in the visual pathways so that an individual can see things that she didn't see before simply by deploying her attention differently" (Berns, *Iconoclast*: 57).

But when Dr. Berns says that "the frontal cortex reconfigures neural networks in the visual pathways," he is not talking about the ability of the individual to exert mental effort (thinking) that results in the stimulation of neural networks in the frontal cortex. What he is saying is that *the frontal cortex deploys the attention of the individual differently*, not that the individual elects to deploy their attention differently. This idea that the brain rather than the person has efficacy in human action, is known formally as materialism. It is the viewpoint that every event in the universe is the result of previous causal and inevitable physical events set in motion at the dawn of time. Materialists hold that the biological, physiological, and electro-chemical events in our brains are the result of a long chain of causal events that lead back in time into a darkness we can never know. This idea leads directly to the conclusion that man has no free will—no power to direct his actions without constraint by necessity or fate—and that any notion or experience we have of free will, including the idea of free will itself, must be a causally necessitated illusion.

Also, when Dr. Berns says "by simply redeploying" he doesn't really mean it is simple. In the very next sentence, he states: "But it is difficult to do this under business-as-usual conditions."

Therefore, simply deploying is difficult, hence not simple. Which is it? Simple or difficult? Logically, it can't be both. In fact, Dr. Berns is just stringing the reader on. At this point we already know that he thinks it is impossible for someone without an iconoclast brain to be an iconoclast.

Still, Dr. Berns wants to hold out some promise to his readers that he has something to reveal about how to think differently in a world without volition. At least they can learn the attributes that Dr. Berns attributes to iconoclasts and perhaps improve some elements of iconoclastic capabilities should their frontal cortex happen to lead them in that direction.

No Choice But To Choose

Chapter 6

FREE WILL? YOUR BRAIN CAN'T HANDLE FREE WILL

Even with the rapid advances in the scientific understanding of the brain, the fact remains that the functioning of the human brain and the phenomenon of consciousness remains a scientific mystery. As neuroscientist Sam Harris writes in *The Moral Landscape*, "The distinction between consciousness and its contents seems paramount. It is true that we do not understand how consciousness emerges from the unconscious activity of neural networks—or even how it *could* emerge" (Harris, *The Moral Landscape*: 221-223 fn18).

On this matter of how consciousness may have emerged from purely causal antecedents, Michael S. Gazzaniga, the Director of the SAGE Center for the Study of Mind at the University of California, Santa Barbara, and president of the Cognitive Neuroscience Institute, provides some guidance on a theoretical possibility in his book *Who's In Charge?: Free Will and the Science of the Brain* (HarperCollins, 2011). The book is based on his 2009 Gifford Lectures.

What we do know is that the brain is a specific thing with a specific nature, and like everything else that exists, it must function in accordance with its nature and conform to materialistic cause and effect. Consciousness is a natural, not a paranormal, phenomenon. It can't operate beyond the boundaries of its nature.

We also know through introspection that we are directly in contact with reality by means of our consciousness and have the power to control our thinking and the actions we initiate within the limits defined by our nature. As philosopher Dr. Leonard Peikoff writes, "Volition is not an exception to the law of causality but rather is a type of causation." Thus, "In regard to any man-made fact, it is valid to claim that man *has* chosen thus, but it was not inherent in the nature of existence for him to have done so; he could have chosen otherwise." (Leonard Peikoff, "The Analytic-Synthetic Dichotomy," in Ayn Rand, *Introduction to Objectivist Epistemology*, 2nd Ed.: 110).

Given the long history of the issue of determinism versus indeterminism in philosophy, Dr. Peikoff indicates his preference for the phrase *self-determinism* rather than free will. Determinism is wrong, he notes, because "you have the choice to think or not, and that in turn determines your actions and emotions and so on…. Indeterminism is also wrong – there is cause and effect; free will is not a violation of cause and effect but rather a *form* of causality." The best description, says Dr. Peikoff, is not "Everything is inevitable, there's no choice," or "There is no law; the world is chance," but rather, "the world is lawful, everything has a cause, but in the case of human action, the cause is certain choices that we ourselves make, free choices, which govern the resulting stream of events" (Leonard Peikoff, *Understanding Objectivism: A Guide to Learning Ayn Rand's Philosophy*, ed. Michael S. Berliner: New American Library, New York, 2012: 285-286).

The key here is that *the fact of causation does not entail the repudiation of free will* (or self-determinism). It is this point that is the impregnable barrier for the determinists/materialists. They believe that because consciousness is causal, so too must be all aspects of the phenomenon, including the content of consciousness and our ability to assert *any* control upon our consciousness.

Take, for example, neuroscientist Bruce Hood, the Director of the Bristol Cognitive Development Centre at the University of Bristol, and a faculty professor at Harvard. Like Dr. Harris, Dr. Hood believes that free will is an illusion and a "logical impossibility." "To me," he says, "the problem of free will is a logical impasse – we cannot choose the factors that ultimately influence what we do and think."[2]

The challenge for science is to explain the processes by which free will arises and operates, not to explain it away or deny its existence by asserting that because scientific knowledge is currently lacking, volitional consciousness and free will is therefore a logical impossibility. Our direct experience confirms its veridicality, which must negate any "logical impossibility." Of what use can it be to rely on logic – the art of non-contradictory identification – if logic conflicts with reality? Reality makes a mockery of "materialist logic." In popular business parlance, one could say reality eats materialistic logic for breakfast.

---

[2] Quoted in Sam Harris, "The Illusion of the Self: An Interview with Bruce Hood," www.samharris.org/blog/item/the-illusion-of-the-self2, May 22, 2012. Accessed September 23, 2017.

That which exists cannot be a logical impossibility. The fault is not with reality. The fault is with an error in logical thinking that fails to properly account for reality. Logic cannot refute the primacy of existence.

The phenomenon of volition is commonly talked about by metaphorically breaking the single entity of the brain into two pieces—*brain* and *mind*—while recognizing that both are the same entity viewed from different perspectives (physical/consciousness). The ability to think and act based on choices we make is what is referred to as *free will*. The *Oxford English Dictionary* defines free will as "the power of acting without the constraint of necessity or fate; the ability to act of one's own direction."

Free will is a completely natural phenomenon and does not entail that our mind is separate from our body, that our brain is separate from our mind, that our thoughts and actions are uncaused or random or free from the nature of our brains, nor that there is a "self" inside of us operating the controls, nor that mind requires the existence of a higher consciousness or is the embodiment of our soul. We must always remember that what we are talking about is selective aspects of a whole living person.

It is evident that underlying Dr. Berns' prognostications about iconoclasts is a basic premise and message: humans are biological creatures of material cause and effect; and biology as it relates to the brain deterministically rules over our behavior and controls and determines the electro-chemical occurrences that we call thinking. Where Dr. Berns goes too far is in his implied denial of volition and free will wrapped up in the counter-factual claim that the *brain* deterministically *controls* our thinking via an infinite regressive causal chain.

What seems more likely is that consciousness and the human form of conceptual thinking is made possible by, and is also constrained by, material cause and effect occurring in our brains that we do not yet understand and may never understand.

Not all neuroscientists agree with Dr. Berns' interpretation of the facts and the logic of his argument in defense of determinism.

Dr. Gazzaniga rejects the validity of the scientific argument put forth by anti-free will advocates, such as Dr. Berns, and Dr. Sam Harris.

Dr. Gazzaniga summarizes the logic of the general argument put forth by neuroscientists to defend their conclusion that free will is an illusion as follows:

(1) The brain enables the mind and the brain is a physical entity; (2) The physical world is determined, so our brains must also be determined; (3) If our brains are determined, and if the brain is the necessary and sufficient organ that enables the mind, then we are left with the belief that the thoughts that arise from our mind also are determined; (4) Thus, free will is an illusion, and we must revise our concepts of what it means to be personally responsible for our actions. Put differently, the concept of free will has no meaning. The concept of free will was an idea that arose before we knew all this stuff about how the brain works, and we should get rid of it. (Gazzaniga, *Who's In Charge?*: 129)

Dr. Gazzaniga goes on to assess the premises of this "causal chain claim" from the parochial and limited perspective of the neuroscience paradigm:

> There is no disagreement among the neuro-scientists about the first claim, that the brain enables the mind in some unknown way and the brain is a physical entity. Claim 2, however, has become a loose link and is under attack. Many physicists are no longer sure that the physical world is predictably determined because the nonlinear mathematics of complex systems does not allow exact predictions of future states. Now we have claim 3 (that our thoughts are determined) on shaky ground. Although some neuroscientists think we may prove that specific neuronal firing patterns will produce specific thoughts and that they are predetermined, none has a clue about what the deterministic rules would be for a nervous system in action. I think that we are facing the same conundrum that physics dealt with when they assumed Newton's laws were universal. The laws are not universal to all levels of organization. It depends which level of organization you are describing, and new rules apply when higher levels emerge. Quantum mechanics are the rules for atoms. Newton's laws are the rules for objects, and one couldn't completely predict the other. So, the question is whether we can take what we know from the micro level of neurophysiology about neurons and neurotransmitters and come up with a determinist model to predict conscious thoughts, the outcomes of brains, or psychology. Or even more problematic is the outcome with the encounter of three brains. Can we derive the macro story from the micro story? I do not think so.

I do not think that brain-state theorists, those neural reductionists who hold that every mental state is identical to some as-yet-undiscovered neural state, will ever be able to demonstrate it. I think conscious thought is an emergent property. That doesn't explain it; it simply recognizes its reality or level of abstraction, like what happens when software and hardware interact, that mind is a somewhat independent property of brain while simultaneously being wholly dependent upon it. I do not think it possible to build a complete model of mental function from the bottom up. (Gazzaniga, *Who's In Charge?*: 129-130)

Returning to Dr. Berns, he is very careful to use language that avoids expressions that outright imply that people have volitional control over their conscious thoughts – that they can freely choose between two or more possible alternatives – and therefore are capable of exercising free will. Nonetheless, he needs to allow for at least some small possibility of free will in order to successfully uphold his claim that iconoclasts have the ability to engage in an act of thinking, which is necessary to differentiate them from non-iconoclasts, and show that iconoclasts think differently.

To help explain why some people are iconoclasts and others are not, Dr. Berns' informs us that the vast majority of individuals are too weak and timid to exercise volitional choice, thereby preventing them from having such a choice. To think and act, says Dr. Berns, is to engage in a noble activity because it requires an act of bravery that few people are able to muster. This leads Dr. Berns to assert that while we may have an inherent but latent capacity for volitional choice, we have no free will unless our brains are structured in such a way that we are able to *choose* free will.

Dr. Berns would like the reader to agree with this contrived view of human nature based on his interpretation of the results of a social psychology experiment by Solomon Asch in the 1950s, conducted with students in a university lab. In essence, the experiment studied the inclination of students to bow to peer pressure, to see if they would select the right answer to a problem or go along with the wrong answer agreed to by actors pretending to be fellow students. He writes: "If we grant that we are all a bit reticent at times to stand up for our personal opinions, this leaves the door open to act as individuals when we choose. It is a noble grasp for free will. But – and this is the kicker – we must be brave enough…. Even in a neutral laboratory setting, most people are not that brave." (Berns, *Iconoclast*: 92).

Do you suppose that you might be brave enough to stick with and defend an answer you know to be correct, and thereby withstand peer pressure exerted by strangers to select a multiple choice answer you knew to be wrong, had you participated in Dr. Asch's experiments on social pressure? Dr. Berns thinks not: "[People] might think that they could decide, for whatever reason, whether to go along or not. But what if that is wrong, and we do not have as much free will as we'd like to think? What if groups of people change how we see the world? Then we are dealing with a much more pernicious form of conformity: a form of conformity we might not even be aware of and one that dooms the would-be iconoclast before he even knows it." (Berns, *Icono-clast*: 92-93).

All that is required to establish free will is that the participants had the ability to make a choice and did so. Dr. Berns ignores the underlying fact that the ability to choose freely is an inescapable underlying premise of the Asch experiment. Without the presumption of free will, the experiment is meaningless and basing any conclusions on the experiment is meaningless. What it attempts to study is the influence of peer pressure on the choices people make under the explicit premise that people are capable of making choices. To interpret the results as a repudiation of free will is patently absurd. It is an example of a logical fallacy known as the "fallacy of the stolen concept" which entails explicitly relying on a concept to make one's argument, then denying the validity of the concept one depended on. Here Dr. Berns tries to use the conclusions of an experiment that entails free will to raise skeptical questions about the existence of free will. If people don't have free will, then using an experiment that entails free will as empirical evidence to deny free will entails "stealing the concept" of free will on the part of Dr. Berns.

Also note that free will either exists as an attribute of a conceptual faculty, or it does not. It is a question of fact, not a matter of degree, as in "we may not have as much of it [i.e., free will] as we'd like to think" or that some people have more of it than do others. It's not a quality that comes and goes by some mysterious and unknowable materialistic mechanism.

To demonstrate that iconoclasts are unlike most people in that they are capable of overcoming their fears to exert free will, Dr. Berns discusses civil rights icon Martin Luther King Jr. and notes that in his courage and leadership "we begin to see clues about how the individual must invoke conscious, rational thought processes to control fear" (Berns, *Iconoclast*: 99).

What Dr. Berns fails to acknowledge is that *all* people begin to teach their children conscious, rational thought processes at a very early age because humans possess consciousness and a proclivity for learning as an aspect of their nature. In the real world, the application of conscious thinking is normal and at the root of psychological health. That volitional thinking is *invoked* and exercised to control fear by a sheer act of will or by acting to improve our environment and make it less fear-evoking is just another concrete instance demonstrating that volitional consciousness entails and is inseparable from free will. Volitional thinking is what enables goal-directed human action— always and everywhere.

It is clear that Dr. Berns is trying to compile enough circumstantial evidence to substantiate the idea that only those with iconoclastic brains have free will, i.e., the ability to control their cognitive capabilities and apply their thinking to solve problems linking efficacious means to the achievement of desired ends. Iconoclasts are like the proverbial one-eyed man in the land of the blind. In Dr. Berns paradigm as a "neuroeconomist," the brain is a separate entity that controls us apart from any illusionary desires and volitional self-control we may feel. For example, he writes, "in many people the brain would rather avoid activating the fear system and just change perception to conform with the social norm" (p. 97). In Dr. Berns' description of the world the brain just does what it does based on a causal sequence of unknowable but unavoidable electrochemical neural events.

In layman's terms, what Dr. Berns is trying hard to sell is that we exist as biological machines compelled by the molecules and electro-chemical forces we are made of to move as we do through the time of our lives. It's as if we are in some bizarre zombie movie in which we are composed of two independent parts – brain and body – melded into one entity, where our body is controlled by our brain and made to do its bidding, blindly following along the path that our brain compels us to take – unless we are one of the lucky few endowed with an iconoclastic brain. He provides no compelling evidential reasons to accept this ancient fiction, first put forth around 500 BC by a school of Greek philosophers known as Atomists.

We are the exact opposite of the fictional zombie, which is why we see the zombie as a fictional construct and not an accurate scientific representation of ourselves. Our brains are hard-wired to make us information-gathering, concept-forming, solution-seeking sentient beings, not passive stimulus-response automatons. We must exercise our volition to assert control over the intensity of our mental focus if we are to put to use the integrative functioning of our brains in support of our lives.

In contrast to free will, determinism means that man has no actual freedom and responsibility because all of his actions result from purely causal materialistic forces that compel his motions and movings. If true, the experience of free will, responsibility, the formation of values and our emotional responses to real-world events, can only be, and must be, an illusion of the brain. It would mean that whatever a person does, he had to do. Whatever a person believes, he had to believe. Whatever a person thinks, he had to think. Whatever a person values, he had to value. Whatever a person feels, he had to feel. For those who deny free will, the mental acts of thinking, learning, believing, valuing, feeling, etc., are all explained away as experiential illusions. Any discussion of such things that do not exist can only be incoherent hallucinatory ramblings. In such a world there can be no difference between mental health and insanity. There is only non-normative materialistic brain activity.

To have a purpose is to act in the present to bring about some end in the future. Determinism, if true, would preclude objectivity in making choices. If we have no free will – no control over our thoughts and actions – then we can have no control over the content of our "knowledge," and cannot strive for further clarification and additional knowledge. The act of striving to discern knowledge and truth from supposition and falsehood requires volitional choice and would thereby negate and be incompatible with the validity of determinism.

If determinism is true, there could be no new discoveries or advances in knowledge. Where would such knowledge come from? Would it be self-generated by deterministic means in human brains in the absence of active thinking? Can electrical discharges in a brain that lacks volition create knowledge, form and utilize concepts, and move a body to act to obey the laws of the natural universe to achieve future goals? For determinists to arbitrarily assert that *this* describes reality is absurd. To advocate such things in all seriousness as the way the natural world works is demonstrably false.

It is clear that if man has no free will, then there could be no knowledge, no science, no innovation, no industry, no civilization, and none of the myriad things that civilization depends on and requires like: language, education, morality, mathematics, farming, engineering, factories, bridges, oil refineries, sewage systems, pencils, printing presses, accounting systems, microchips, computer devices, modern medicine and pharmaceuticals, electromagnetic imaging technology, courts of law, economic science, etc., as well as the countless incremental discoveries and innovations that made each of these possible. It is a unique human ability to form and use linguistic concepts ultimately derived from direct perception of reality that makes the retention and use of knowledge and its growth over time possible. Determinists put forth no theories to explain how we (and they) come to know and act, and to explain away what we (and they) directly experience. Any valid theory requires reference to the senses and applied consciousness.

It is our ability to validate conclusions and apply our knowledge and expand it that allows for efficacious human action and the progress of civilization. If determinism was true and it followed that thinking is an illusion, we would have no way of judging truth and falsehood, including the validity of determinism and its claims, and therefore no way of validating the truth status of the concept of determinism.

The human quest for knowledge including all philosophical, moral, and scientific questions would be meaningless for a determinist who believes he or she possesses validated evidence that the thinking and actions of individuals are not within their volitional control. The individual would only think about them because the brain engaged itself in a particular causal event set in motion in the dark recesses of the formation of the universe. On this premise, any notion that we are capable of directing our thoughts through a logical process that leads from observations to conclusions would have to be an illusion. Our first-hand experience that we have the ability to utilize our consciousness to drive action, or that our thinking is purposefully self-directed, would have to be an illusion or hallucination.

As you proceed along this path, you can see the absurdity of the claim that free will (or self-determinism) is false. The claim to know that choice is an illusion itself entails confirmed knowledge of what it would be like to possess free will. Orangutans don't look at humans and contemplate what their lives would be like if only they possessed the faculty of concept formation and higher-level thinking. To comprehend such a thing already entails its possession. Likewise, to contrast the illusion of free will to the actual thing is to already possess the true item.

The facts of reality overwhelmingly refute the validity of determinism as it relates to human consciousness. Dr. Berns' solution to this problem is to suppose that all new knowledge springs forth from the brains of iconoclasts – or more precisely, from those with iconoclastic brains. Those with iconoclastic brains are "somehow" able to break through the zombie-like mental state as exceptions to the deterministic cognitive processes and existence of the masses of humanity.

Had he taken a more philosophic and reasoned approach to his work and his thesis, Dr. Berns should have seen that the very existence of electromagnetic imaging technology is sufficient empirical evidence to *refute* the theory of determinism. Each of a long chain of discoveries by individuals through history that eventually resulted in the creation and use of electromagnetic imaging technology that forms the central tool of Dr. Berns' work was the result of free-thought and human agency of which every conscious man, woman and child is capable. Free will is introspectively obvious in my choice of which words to write down on paper to express my thought. Could one write poetry, or prose, or compose music without free will? Could Dr. Berns write his book, or conduct research, or develop and deliver lectures, debate with students and grade their papers without free will? What would be the purpose of grading a paper in which the student could not have written otherwise and Dr. Berns could not have assigned a grade other than that which was assigned?

If his theory is to have any credibility as something to be seriously considered by practical people of reason—by entrepreneurs, business professionals, and organizational leaders—he requires that we *believe* so.

Chapter 7

THE FALSE DICHOTOMY OF BRAIN VERSUS MIND

It appears that for many in the field of neuroscience the phenomenon of the human mind is weakly engaged to exert free will in a constant yet futile war against the brain. Free will doesn't entail that the motivating reasons for our thinking, choices, and actions are without cause. Free will names the fact that humans have the ability to control their mental focus and to act purposefully to imagine and create pathways that lead to future desired ends. Free will entails that the brain is part of a bodily system that engages in a natural phenomenon that allows it to exert some aspects of willful control over its own functioning. Free will entails ends-pursuing action, i.e., teleology.

Of course, the capabilities of the human brain are determined by the inherent nature of what humans and brains are. They can only do what is within their nature. They can only do that of which they are capable. The same is true of people, each of whom has a brain. People have the unique ability to exert considerable control over the use of certain elements of their consciousness related to thinking and action. People are capable of imagining future outcomes and taking action in the present based on knowledge learned in the past. We can choose to put our minds to use doing the mental work required to solve problems, or we can choose to avoid doing so. Either way, people must make choices of their own volition and can act or refrain from doing so based on the choices they make. This is an irrefutable fact about human brains.

The validity of free will and agency underlies the very process of thinking and goal-directed behavior in humans. It is self-evident and can be verified by our own observations based on the evidence of our senses and our own introspection of formulating ends and successfully planning and acting to achieve them. People are employed in jobs and paid salaries to do exactly this every day. Human life requires problem solving, and problem solving requires the weighing of means and ends and the mental act of decision-making within a context of values and abilities, i.e., human life requires free will.

It is important not to confuse the fact that we have motivating reasons for our actions – which is compatible with free will – with the determinist thesis that we are incapable of making non-illusory choices and acting on them. Motives are a type of cause in that they indicate reasons in the form of underlying values held that explain particular actions. Motives have causes, but we have the ability to formulate motives, think about them, change them, and then act on them or elect not to act on them, now or in the future. Action is the end result of a volitional process that converts urges into desires into plans into action. We can take action for good reasons or for bad reasons, at an appropriate time or not, depending on the motives we formulate. At any point we can sustain the process of action to its conclusion, or not.

These facts lead to a logical paradox inherent in any pro-determinism argument: the act of formulating and making the argument to deny free will requires an act of free will, thereby negating the validity of the anti-free will argument. In other words, free will as a philosophic or scientific doctrine pertaining to the nature of people and their ability to think and act is axiomatic, and its negation in the form of determinism as it relates to human thinking and action is self-refuting. As the rock band Rush sing in their hit song *Free Will*, "If you choose not to decide, you still have made a choice." There's no escaping free will.

As Dr. Locke discusses in his book *The Illusion of Determinism*, the brain makes consciousness possible. When the brain ceases to function so does consciousness. Consciousness is an axiom and self-evident primary because the experience of awareness can't be deduced from anything else. That you experience things directly is the direct evidence that you are conscious of those things. To claim "I am not conscious" is not only a contradiction, it is a self-evident refutation of the claim itself.

Dr. Berns rejects such claims as irrelevant and holds the opposite view: he alleges that determinism is axiomatic because all events have prior physical causes. And yet he notes that there are some people who appear to possess extraordinary capabilities for which the notion of determinism can't account. By assuming a reductionist approach to human behavior in which all human actions are caused by a prior chain of causal materialistic activity in the brain, Dr. Berns is unable to explain human achievement that rises above the mundane, i.e., the achievements of those he refers to as iconoclasts. His solution to the perceived determinist paradox is to build a circumstantial case that iconoclasts, and only iconoclasts, possess at least some semblance of free will, thereby proving that their brains are different.

In this way, Dr. Berns uses determinist language to describe and explain away human volition as an illusion, while making the softer claim that some people have brains that are wired for free will. This is evidenced by his comments that with regards to free will, most people are too weak of mind to overcome innate biological resistance to its use; that for all intents-and-purposes, the majority of humanity are incapable of free will; and that only a small subset of people have brains that allow for free will to be such that it rises to the level of being meaningful in their lives. For most of us—those of us with brains incapable of overcoming the barriers to utilizing our free will—free will is an illusion. We may be deceived by our brains into thinking we possess it, but according to Dr. Berns, we don't.

While Dr. Berns tries to sidestep the implications of biological determinism by asserting a weak compromise to free will when his theory enters into a frontal assault with reality, the deterministic language he uses to describe reality reveals an anti-free will ideological bias. Consider this description by Dr. Berns of what we commonly refer to as thinking (thinking being the ability of humans to control their consciousness through the application of logic and the integration of knowledge to solve problems): "When other individuals render opinions [about visual stimuli], the brain readily incorporates these opinions and changes its interpretation of visual information. It is far too inefficient for an individual brain to make repeated guesses about what it is seeing, and when offered the opinion of other people...the brain will readily assimilate this information into its own interpretation and perception" (Berns, *Iconoclast*: 101).

In other words, as humans, we have little or no control over our opinions and conclusions, which means we have little control over the thinking we do or don't do and the way we integrate new information with our existing knowledge to form conclusions and opinions using reason and logic. Rather, the opinions of others, which are likewise formed by brains mindlessly incorporating the opinions of others in an ongoing regression of transmission of information, write themselves onto our brain and change our concept of reality. It's akin to a biological assertion by an anthropomorphized brain that "all your mind are belong to us" and resistance is futile.[3]

Determinist arguments are currently popular in our culture with psychiatrists, neuroscientists, biologists, and pop psychologists leading the charge with a frontal assault on human consciousness, free will, and personal responsibility. There is wide-spread and growing belief in society that our preferences and choices are genetically determined. Dr. Berns is joined by fellow neuroscientist Sam Harris in claiming that free will is an illusion of human consciousness.

Sam Harris is best known as the author of *The End Of Faith, The Moral Landscape,* and more recently *Free Will*, and, ironically, for his moral

---

[3] Reference is to a 2001 popular Internet meme: https://youtu.be/jQE66WA2s-A

crusade along with Richard Dawkins and others in favour of a scientific worldview as against religious mysticism as a valid methodology for acquiring and validating knowledge. It is commonly accepted that a fundamental requirement for a normative morality is the ability of people to make choices amongst alternatives relative to an objective standard in order to pursue their own well-being. Without free will, there can be no moral principles, no virtues (including the virtues of rationality and justice), no individual responsibility and accountability, etc. And yet in his book *The Moral Landscape,* Dr. Harris goes further than Dr. Berns by explicitly and unequivocally asserting a discovered knowledge that humans do *not* have free will.

In a section headed "The Illusion of Free Will" Dr. Harris writes: "From [the experiential] point of view, you tend to feel that you are the source of your own thoughts and actions. *You* decide what to do and not to do. You seem to be an agent acting of your own free will. As we will see, however, this point of view cannot be reconciled with what we know about the human brain" (*The Moral Landscape*, p. 102). In his blog on May 30, 2011, Dr. Harris reiterates this perspective, writing: "In fact, the concept of free will is a non-starter, both philosophically and scientifically. There is simply no description of mental and physical causation that allows for this freedom that we habitually claim for ourselves and ascribe to others. Understanding this would alter our view of morality in some respects, but it wouldn't destroy the distinction between right and wrong, or good and evil."[4]

---

[4] http://www.samharris.org/blog/item/morality-without-free-will/

It is true that if we predefine right and wrong, good and evil, based on intuition or feelings rather than demonstrated evidence tied directly to the facts of reality, then we can observe behaviour and describe whether it conforms to accepted norms. But without existential freedom to make choices there is no possibility of applying a proper philosophic methodology to define and delineate the proper boundaries of normative human behavior, teach it to others, and hold people accountable for the choices and actions they take in pursuit of their own well-being. Freedom of choice and action and moral responsibility and personal accountability go hand in glove. If you believe free will is an illusion, then you are logically committed to normative ethics as being equally illusive. If, that is, you are bounded by rationality.

It may be true as Dr. Harris asserts that given our current state of knowledge, "there is no description of mental and physical causation" at the level of the brain that accounts for free will. But to conclude thereby that the choices we make every moment of our lives to stay alive and improve our well-being are mere illusions is an egregious error in logic and abuse of scientific authority.

Dr. Harris suffers from the same confusions as Dr. Berns. Any argument Dr. Harris makes about knowledge depends on the axiom of human consciousness and human volition, i.e., free will. As we have seen, this is axiomatic and doesn't require a scientific explanation or proof. It is impossible to provide a proof of free will by some means that doesn't already require free will. The ability to perceive entities, form concepts, and discover and apply a methodology to gain knowledge is ostensive prima facie evidence that humans possess a voli-tional consciousness, and as a corollary, possess free will. A mere assertion that free will can't be *explained* "scientifically" at the level of a deterministic causal chain of physical events is not a valid reason to deny its existence as a metaphysically real phenomenon.

It is an even more egregious error in reasoning and logic to claim that our knowledge of the human brain proves that free will is an illusion! What this conclusion should suggest to anyone that has reached it is that they are mistaken about what scientists truly know about the human brain. To claim that one has discovered knowledge about the human brain that requires the denial of free will is prima facie evidence of erroneous knowledge, not a justification to throw out the existence of free will.

What is more perplexing about Dr. Harris's deterministic position is that he explicitly accepts what is assuredly true: the reality of human consciousness and its ability to arise from purely materialistic causes. Yet he denies that this inexplicable natural phenomenon could include free will. He writes: "The distinction between consciousness and its contents seems paramount. It is true that we do not understand how consciousness emerges from the unconscious activity of neural networks – or even how it could emerge...It seems to me that progress on this front does not require that we solve the 'hard problem' of consciousness (or that it even admit of a solution). When comparing mental states, the reality of human consciousness is a given. We need not understand how consciousness relates to the behavior of atoms to investigate how emotions like love, compassion, trust, greed, fear, and anger differ (and interact) in neurological terms" (Harris, *The Moral Landscape*: 221-222 n. 18).

On the one hand Dr. Harris admits and accepts that the existence of human consciousness is undeniable even though there is no current "scientific" explanation for it and perhaps never will be. On the other hand, he believes he has legitimate "scientific" grounds based on what we know today about the brain to deny that human consciousness can be volitional in its nature – that *every* choice we make to sustain our lives and exert our will is necessarily an illusion; that we survive as individuals and prosper as a civilization by purely mechanistic means, like some mathematical algorithm creating an ever-expanding fractal on a computer screen.

If this is the case, I think he owes his readers an explanation as to why the emotions he cites – love, compassion, trust, greed, fear, and anger – are not also illusions. Also, It seems to follow that if free will is an illusion, then it must be meaningless to ever assert that we are forced to act against our will. Our negative emotions and feelings of being exploited, coerced, oppressed, cheated, threatened, etc., all of which pertain to restrictions on acting in ways we deem desirable as compared to alternatives that we do not voluntarily choose to pursue, must also be mere illusions that should be ignored. To deny free will is to undermine the foundation for life sustaining concepts like liberty and freedom, and the moral virtues of rationality, honesty, integrity, independence, justice, productiveness and pride.

Such undermining based on an embrace of the illusion of *determinism* is inherently destructive to valid thought and meaningful action.

Chapter 8

THE DETERMINIST PARADOX?

In the article "Zeno's Paradox and the Problem of Free Will," Phil Molé discusses whether determinists are looking at the problem of free will correctly and how "deterministic laws do not preclude the possibility of free will" (eSkeptic, April 27, 2011).[5] Mr. Molé proposes that the problem of free will is based on conceptual confusions in which its defenders mistakenly accept the premises of a paradox. What they should do instead is reject the paradox because it conflicts with what we know to be true based on direct observation through introspection and extrospection. He writes: "What if, just as in Zeno's paradox, there is nothing truly paradoxical going on in the realm of free will after all? What if our actions could remain genuine acts of will *and* outcomes of a complex chain of causality....?"

"When we talk about free will and determinism," he writes, "we immediately confront a series of conflicts between seemingly contradictory terms. When we ask if a deterministic universe implies the absence of freedom, we seem to encounter a conflict between the concepts of cause and choice...."

What Mr. Molé proposes is that we are forced into a confusing paradox by how we pose the question "How can man have free will?"

---

[5] http://www.skeptic.com/eskeptic/11-04-27

I agree. And if we are talking about a metaphysical question, I would go one step further. The question itself is illegitimate because it is inherently illogical and contradicts reality. It's like asking: "How can acorns grow into oak trees?" If we try to hold to our observational knowledge that when we plant an acorn it grows into an oak tree, while at the same time denying this possibility because the process seems mysterious and we cannot explain how it came to be this way, we put ourselves in an impossible situation. The same is true with regards to the question of free will. To pose the question "how can man have free will?" already requires free will. But if one rejects ostensive validation as proper evidence for the existence of free will and instead demands some "proof" beyond our comprehension because the idea of free will entails a logical contradiction, then one puts oneself in an impossible situation. It is a contradiction to attempt to prove free will without already presuming free will as part of the process of proof. To try to hold to this contradiction creates a paradox by posing the non-existence of free will as a valid premise in the first place.

For example, if it is true that in order to survive every living organism must possess the ability to control its actions at some primitive or advanced level, then the denial of this fact would lead us to erroneous conclusions about the nature of living organisms. The same is true with regards to the study of man. If man is capable of choice and one studies man as if he is incapable of choice, then all of one's conclusions where motives and actions are involved will be invalid. To study the thinking and actions of man as is required in any of the social sciences (e.g., economics, psychology, history, politics, law, anthropology, etc.) while denying free will and holding to the metaphysical impossibility of human choice is to fail to properly study man. Under the assumption that man is incapable of making choices, there is nothing that can be learned and nothing to be understood. If choice is an illusion, no normative conclusions about goal-directed means and ends can be derived to further serve man's well-being in the pursuit of life, liberty and happiness.

That we pose the question as to whether man has free will entails an unstated underlying premise that the determinists must hold to be true, namely that man can sustain his life as a biological entity while lacking a mechanism or ability to make real choices amongst alternative paths that control and direct his actions toward life-sustaining, ends. Is human life possible under such conditions, as the determinists imply?

The facts indicate that it is not. All living organisms require the ability to adapt in real time to their environments in a constant pursuit of survival. Man, as a species, is unique in that his means of sustaining life resides in conscious, volitional, long-range choices.

The Determinist Paradox is created by juxtaposing what we know to be necessarily true— that man is a being of volitional consciousness— with a contradictory proposition: that the choices we make are given to us by fate and are mere illusions because science pertains to the discovery of deterministic laws of nature, and science can't account for or countenance occurrences in the brain that don't result from and entail strictly deterministic and materialist cause and effect.

Neuroscientists hold that the brain controls all major human biological activity and do not believe that human activity can occur without physical causal antecedents. A great many of them do not accept that humans can be the prime movers of their own consciousness or the cause of their own choices. From this they *deduce* that free will must be an illusion based on the premise that free will is incompatible with the strictly causal laws of nature. Because nothing incompatible with the strictly causal laws of nature can exist in nature, the conclusion is reached that therefore free will does not exist. If this conclusion is true then free will must be an existential impossibility, and any felt experience of choice can only be explained as a naturalistic and causal psychological delusion.

On the other hand, if free will manifests itself as a phenomenon of nature and natural laws, as it does, then there must be a natural and causal explanation, even if science is not yet (or perhaps ever?) able to explain it.

To summarize, the Deterministic Paradox arises when what appears to be a serious inquiry questioning the legitimacy of free will is pursued, and when that inquiry must, by the nature of it being an inquiry, entail the very act of free will that it purports to question and to ultimately deny as real. This is an example of the logical fallacy philosopher Ayn Rand identified as *concept stealing*. Concept stealing is the act of using a higher-level concept while denying the roots and existence of the more basic concepts on which it depends. Consider that to presume the validity of determinism and ask, "how can man have free will if all brain activity is causal?" entails the existence of free will in the act of asking and attempting to answer. This leads to the seemingly paradoxical conclusion that the determinist must necessarily validate free will when putting forth any argument for its non-existence.

While scientists may not be able to explain the mechanism of free will, the questions as to *whether* we have free will, and *how* it is that we have free will, are two different questions. As Sam Harris notes, we may never be able to answer the *how* of consciousness. Still, the scientific problem of discovering a causal explanation for the mechanism of free will and human consciousness does not provide any legitimate grounds to deny existence to those as yet unknown mechanisms.

To be aware of existence requires consciousness. The purpose of consciousness is to ensure constant generation of action to sustain the life of a living entity by means of choice. To have the capability to make a choice amongst alternative actions is to have free will.

Whether we have free will is answerable by direct evidence through conscious awareness. Its veracity does not depend on an explanation of the phenomenon of consciousness. *How* we have free will is a question for science to answer. Some people refuse to accept ostensible evidence from the senses or direct introspection as valid. Instead they choose to deny reality unless it can be proved by means of empirical observation and deductive logic.

Zeno thought that his logic was flawless in demonstrating the impossibility of motion. But why should we accept that Achilles must continually slow down rather than keep a steady pace in moving forward? Why must we try to resolve the paradox from the inside on Zeno's terms by accepting a dubious set of conditions and premises when we *know* that Achilles can easily outrun the tortoise?

Such puzzles and paradoxes are interesting and form the central theme in many fantasy-fiction stories. The paradox of time travel is on display in movies such as *Back To The Future;* or the paradox of predestination in movies such as *Minority Report*; or the paradox of a living incorporeal soul in ghost movies such as *The Others* or the Harry Potter movies, etc. These movies are entertaining because they weave unusual puzzles and paradoxes into the narrative. But ultimately they are unsatisfying because they must also leave the paradox unresolved without an acceptable logical explanation of the impossible events underlying the story. We admire the escapism of such stories *because* of their fantastic and imaginative qualities as fiction, not because they are a valid representation of reality.

The same sense of dissatisfaction underlies the denial of free will and the assertion that all choices are merely an illusion. Why should we accept the dubious set of conditions and premises put forth in the Determinist Paradox (that the choices we make are not true choices and are just an illusion) when we know from our own experience that it just isn't so? Why should we allow ourselves to be intimidated by purportedly scientific claims on the part of authority figures by virtue of their Ph.Ds. and accept the assertion that we are scientifically ignorant because we accept our senses and consciousness as valid means to gain knowledge of reality? Why should we accept that our judgment is flawed by the nature of our being, but not the judgment of the scientists or philosophers who tell us it is so?

Phil Molé brings these threads together, writing: "Just as modern determinists intimidate us by speaking of infinite chains of causes precluding our freedom, Zeno intimidated his audience by showing how infinite numbers of small increments rendered motion impossible. What if, just as in Zeno's paradox, there is nothing truly paradoxical going on in the realm of free will after all? What if our actions could remain genuine acts of will and outcomes of a complex chain of causality...?"

In the end, Dr. Harris, like fellow neuroscientist Dr. Berns and others who embrace the Determinist Paradox, seems unable to reconcile the undeniable fact that man possesses free will with the assumptions of neuroscience as a science. Both Dr. Harris and Dr. Berns take as prima facie evidence against free will the inability of a positivist approach to prove free will at the level of molecular activity in the brain combined with a theoretical construct of how the brain *should* work.

In terms of his scientific methodology, when Dr. Harris identifies a contradiction between reality and speculative theory, he appears too eager to discard reality. He appears to be caught in a materialistic/ deterministic paradigm related to neuroscience that assumes it can study the mysteries of human consciousness on the same deterministic assumptions that apply when studying other deterministic natural events like weather patterns, seismology, and the shifting of the tides, when it can't. As noted earlier, and to be further discussed later, the social sciences require a separate and distinct methodology because they require the study of a unique class of entities capable of initiating aspects of their own behavior. Of course, if one rejects the evidence that such creatures exist, then one can smugly elect to ignore the proper methodology for studying human action.

One of the studies that Dr. Harris cites as evidence that free will is an illusion is research by physiologist Benjamin Libet. According to Harris, Libet has demonstrated that "activity in the brain's motor regions can be detected some 350 milliseconds before a person feels that he has decided to move," and that "some 'conscious' decisions can be predicted up to 10 *seconds* before they enter awareness" (Harris, *The Moral Landscape*: 103). Harris concludes: "The truth seems inescapable: I, as the subject of my experience, cannot know what I will next think or do until a thought or intention arises; and thoughts and intentions are caused by physical events and mental stirrings which I am not aware."

The evidence, says Dr. Harris, shows that the brain is causal – that all thinking and "self-generated" action occurs in the brain; the implication is that because all choices must be physically caused, anyone who holds that humans have free will is out of step with the demonstrated facts of science.

It is true that like all things the brain is an entity of a specific kind with a specific nature and must abide by its nature. That humans make choices is also a fact about human brains and their nature. So is the fact that a choice that is generated and occurs in the brain is itself also a cause that triggers brain activity. Free will does not necessitate the introduction of uncaused causes because to choose (to have volition) is to self-initiate a causal chain of events in the brain. What is unique about people is their ability to initiate such choices and their causal effects. What else could it mean to choose? The question of how it is that we are able to do this is an entirely separate issue from the fact that we are able to do so. The lack of an explanation of the materialistic mechanism by which we have this capability does not overturn or usurp reality.

Interestingly, research psychiatrist and author Jeffery Schwartz and his colleagues offer a different interpretation of Libet's research. They argue that Libet's research shows that people have free will as demonstrated by cognitive "veto power" (see Jeffrey Schwartz, Pablo Gaito & Doug Lennick, "That's The Way We (Used To) Do Things Around Here" in *strategy+business*, Issue 62, Spring 2011).[6] They write:

> In one of the most discussed experiments in the history of neuroscience, preeminent researcher Benjamin Libet used electroencephalographic equipment to measure the brain functions underlying simple finger movements. He discovered that three-tenths of a second before people are aware of the will to move their finger, there is a brain signal related to a desire for finger movement. A person may have the desire to move, but then choose not to move; these two thoughts – the desire and the choice – are separate.

---

[6] http://www.strategy-business.com/article/11109?gko=8928a

Many people believe that their control over their impulses is limited, particularly in the face of such strong emotions as anger, frustration, enthusiasm, or grief. To an extent, that is true, but Libet's work shows that people can always constrain (or choose not to follow) a particular impulse. People may have only limited free will, but they have powerful "free won't."

Schwartz, Gaito and Lennick, contrary to the conclusion reached by neuro-determinists, conclude that Libet's research demonstrates the *existence* of free will. We must note, however, that they are wrong in their formulation of free will: Where there is choice there is free will, full stop.

Because Schwartz, Gaito and Lennick recognize free will, they are able to provide prescriptive guidance to business managers based on neuroscience research. Berns on the other hand provides a pessimistic dead end because he believes that all people, with the exception of iconoclasts, are incapable of exercising free will, making it futile for such persons to even try to pursue their illusory ambitions.

There is irony in Dr. Harris's attempt to deny free will in a book purported to discuss and convince others of the importance of discovering the human values required to live a happy, healthy, and successful life, and choosing to act accordingly. Of course, if we have no free will then we cannot choose to act accordingly. And if we cannot choose or think differently than we do, and control our actions, then we cannot be responsible for our thinking or our actions; we cannot be agents worthy of either moral praise or condemnation. If we cannot choose, our actions cannot be voluntary in the ordinary sense of the word, but rather must be either random or predetermined by physical causal forces emanating from within us but beyond our knowledge and volitional control.

In other places Dr. Harris is explicitly an advocate of moral choice, which leads me to conclude that in his exuberance to deny the "ghost in the machine"—that man's consciousness is dependent on the existence of a god—and to argue for a natural and scientific explanation for free will, he has thrown out the baby with the bath water. He appears to have failed to understand that you cannot properly disintegrate and compartmentalize knowledge in the name of science. Science presupposes categories of philosophy and philosophic axioms that it depends upon and must embrace for its legitimacy, including the existence of human consciousness and its axiomatic corollary, free will. It is an error to claim as Dr. Harris does that man has no free will metaphysically, but that he does epistemologically. Epistemology depends on free will for its discovery, articulation, and validation, which entails that man's capacity for free will exists metaphysically (i.e., in reality, not in a mystical other-worldly sense).

It is a mistake to let the defenders of the Determinist Paradox and enemies of free will define the terms of the debate when those terms are not defined objectively, and when it can be demonstrated that the premises they presume to be true are not true.

There are some puzzles or paradoxes that cannot be properly argued against if you accept as valid their invalid or contradictory premises but are easily refuted when considered from a different perspective. For example, you don't need to discover calculus to resolve Zeno's paradox. You just have to reject the premise in which the paradox is framed and recognize that speed equals distance divided by time. There is nothing that requires us to enter into the world of the paradox without sufficient credible evidence to do so if that means rejecting the sum of our current integrated knowledge of the world.

Chapter 9

HAVE NO FEAR, AN ICONOCLAST IS HERE

Dr. Berns proposes that the absence of fear of failure is a necessary characteristic of being an iconoclast. According to Dr. Berns, for a person to be an iconoclast they must rouse the courage to challenge accepted social wisdom by doing something that others believe cannot be done. The ability to do so, says Dr. Berns, requires that the iconoclast brain be different in kind from the brains possessed by others.

One of the differences Dr. Berns identifies is that non-iconoclast brains are constantly being overwritten by the opinions of others because the non-iconoclast brain cannot refrain from substituting the opinions of others for self-initiated thinking and concept-formation generated experientially and inductively from sense perception. Those in possession of a non-iconoclastic brain are kept blind to reality through some kind of undefined process of deterministic cognitive osmosis: we blindly absorb the opinions of others and act on those opinions under the illusion that we are thinking for ourselves and making choices.

Dr. Berns thus asserts by implication that non-iconoclastic brains are infinitely malleable, bending to the ever-changing kaleidoscopic and ephemeral opinion of "others." Just as only the iconoclastic mind can perceive reality undistorted by the opinions of others, so it is also that only the iconoclastic mind can possess the courage and capability to choose to pursue a goal knowing it is possible that action taken can lead to failure. Dr. Berns writes that "Only the iconoclast resists" the type of perceptual distortion that leads to a fear of failure because only the iconoclast has the ability to ensure that fear of failure doesn't distort "rational" thinking (Berns, *Iconoclast*: 112).

Note that Dr. Berns is claiming far more than the rather mundane and obvious assertion that to be successful an iconoclast must be able to rouse the courage to act with integrity and overcome the fear of what has often amounted to career-threatening and even life-threatening opposition; or that iconoclasts are successful in part because they don't allow their fear of failure to distort their outlook on problem solving.

What is audacious is Dr. Berns' claim for the existence of a preponderance of scientific evidence to support his conclusion that almost all humans are subject to "perceptual distortion" by their nature, which results in an existential fear of failure, and that only iconoclasts have the ability or will to resist this existential fear of failure and perceive reality as it really is.

Chapter 10

THE PURPORTED CLASH BETWEEN REALITY AND "RATIONALITY"

Dr. Berns is following a long tradition of economists and social scientists trying to model theories of human behaviour along the lines of mathematics and physics, where hard causal laws exist. Such models always fail when applied to human behaviour because human beings don't act with the mechanical precision of the molecules of which they are composed. Humans are capable of self-generated action undertaken in pursuit of goals of their own choosing and appropriate for their own unique circumstances.

Physical laws of cause and effect must apply to human biology, but these facts can never undermine the equally factual phenomenon of human volitional consciousness and choice. How humans choose to think and act is left to their own discretion within the confines of what is possible to humans by the nature of the universe. As rational beings, we can assess and weigh dozens of variables consisting of means and ends and values and probabilities and whims and desires over a myriad of temporal divisions by applying or failing to effectively apply our faculty of rationality to the knowledge we have acquired. A science of human action must take this into account and must adopt an appropriate but different methodology than the purely mechanical and materialistic causal paradigm of physics.

Dr. Berns marginalizes human consciousness and the ability of the vast majority of people to think and engage in meaningful action over time. Because of this, he must substitute a different meaning for rationality than the common one to which we are all directly experientially familiar. He must bend reality to suit his purpose and maintain his pseudo-reality.

For Dr. Berns, human rationality has almost nothing to do with real thinking about the real world and one's situation in it, and of making choices and acting to remove impediments to achieving goals and thereby improving one's well-being. Rationality for Dr. Berns is akin to conformity to an artificial man-made mathematical utility model.

According to Dr. Berns, "neuroimaging experiments suggest that the brain does perform calculations similar to" what mid-20th Century mathematicians John Von Neumann and Oskar Morgenstern predicted in a utility theory they put forth in their influential book *The Theory of Games And Economic Behavior*. According to Dr. Berns, Von Neumann and Morgenstern's Expected Utility Theory (EUT) suggests that "when an individual is faced with a decision and must make a choice between competing alternatives, the person chooses the course of action with the greatest expected utility." To calculate expected utility, "you multiply the utility of *every possible outcome* by the probability that it will actually happen. Then you choose the action with the highest EU" (Berns, *Iconoclast*: 113, emphasis added). Rationality for Dr. Berns is choosing the action with the highest Expected Utility, as determined by whoever supposedly determines these things. Failure to choose the action with the highest EU is considered by Dr. Berns to be non-rational, and a failure in human rationality (or a demonstration that humans completely lack rationality).

Dr. Berns indicates that neuroimaging shows that our brains perform these sorts of utility calculations when making decisions. We should not find it surprising that the brain engages in some sort of 'calculation' because the weighing of outcomes is what it means to deliberate when making a decision. Thinking is what people with brains and free will do.

But then Dr. Berns reveals what to him is a startling finding but which should be self-evident: that the "vast majority of people, in fact, do not consciously make decisions" by utilizing Expected Utility Theory. To do so, says Dr. Berns, "requires you to accurately gauge how you will feel about every possible outcome, and calculate the odds of each outcome actually occurring" (Berns, *Iconoclast*: 113).

The truth is that *nobody* utilizes EUT as Dr. Berns defines it because it is humanly impossible to perform a calculus that considers every possible outcome. That *any* human brain is capable of doing this is pure fantasy and an attempt to hold human rationality to a standard that cannot be met, i.e., to a standard that is inhuman. Yet Dr. Berns by implication makes the purportedly factual but fantastic claim that there exists a minority of people who can and do calculate the odds of *every* possible outcome occurring, if not all the time, then at least on a regular basis. (Also note that for Dr. Berns, rationality leaves aside any standard by which we should choose other than "how you will feel," which may not coincide with the option that provides the greatest utility. We will leave aside the moral issue of whether utility is the appropriate standard for making rational choices.)

As humans, we perform mental calculations all of the time in an effort to determine and carry out our life-sustaining requirements, and we do so, as Dr. Berns notes, "even when the person is unaware of it." That's what thinking is, and what human life requires. We should not be surprised that there is some correspondence with a theory developed to describe how we make choices to pursue desired goals – such as EUT – and that neuroimaging may indicate that our brains are actively performing such life-affirming and sustaining calculations. What is surprising is Dr. Berns' claim that our brains perform these EU calculations at a non-conscious level and that our brains are not very good at it: "As it turns out," writes Dr. Berns, "the people who actually do make decisions resembling what EUT predicts are probably the true iconoclasts. Everyone else suffers from a host of perceptual distortions that lead to a cornucopia of decision-making maladies" (Berns, *Iconoclast*: 113).

It's unclear to the reader how Dr. Berns could know from neuroimaging that our brains are always performing EUT-like calculations unconsciously if our choices do not correspond to what EUT would predict. It is arbitrary and therefore meaningless to say our brains go through an expected utility calculation that almost always gives the wrong answer. If we don't get the "right" answer when the theory says we are supposed to, maybe there's something wrong with the theory, not with people or brains. It's like asserting as a theory that humans always make calculations based on the principles of calculus, except that humans aren't very good at calculus and so arrive at the wrong answers. Such a theory is completely arbitrary and without meaning because the conclusion contradicts the premises inherent in the theory. EUT was an attempt to develop a model to help understand and explain the human decision-making process. If the theory doesn't map perfectly to reality, one should acknowledge the limits of the theory and its models rather than redefine reality to fit a theory that was developed in an attempt to describe or represent reality in the first place.

Chapter 11

THE STUDY OF ACTION REQUIRES AN APPROPRIATE METHOD

To try to resolve the contradictions that arise when holding that people do not have free will is like trying to resolve the paradox of time travel we find so often in science fiction movies. Just as it is impossible for a man to go back in time to affect future events in his life and reshape the course of future human history that led to the time travel situation in the first place, so too is it impossible to even comprehend any aspect of human affairs that require goal directed action without accepting that people have, and are able to exert control over, their desires, goals, wills and intentions. To talk of human affairs without acknowledging the veracity of free will and human agency is akin to jabbering incoherently.

In criticizing the reductionist approach taken by many neuroscientists, Daniel James Sanchez writes: "It is not enough to know *that* firing neurons leads to behaviors. For a scientist studying human behavior to practice methodological monism, he would need to know *which* circumstances regarding the firing of neurons would lead to the bodily motions that 'silly folk psychologists' call 'composing a symphony,' and *which* circumstances regarding the firing of neurons would instead lead to the bodily motions that 'silly folk psychologists' call 'reading a book.' So long as we can't accomplish such a mind-boggling feat as that, the only way of studying human affairs that makes sense is by considering humans as acting beings with minds, wills and intentions" (see his essay "Mises on Mind and Method."[7]

The recognition that the study of acting man requires a different methodology than the study of inanimate things and that both are appropriate and necessary in the proper context is commonly referred to as *methodological dualism.*[8]

Methodological dualism recognizes that to be objective, we require a methodology for dealing with the study of human actions and the social sciences that is different from that required when studying the natural sciences.

When scientists reject methodological dualism in favour of the idea that a single experimental method is valid for all scientific study (methodological monism), they are forced to treat human behaviour in the same manner as atoms and weather patterns, i.e., as completely deterministic outcomes resulting from a continuous chain of causal events that leads back in time to some indescribable first cause. It is assumed by those who hold a fully deterministic model of all things, including human action, that every future event is theoretically predictable prior to its occurrence. This viewpoint is known as *positivism* and its adherents as *positivists.*[9]

Positivism flatly denies that any field of inquiry is open for teleological research (research of actions directed towards goals) because science can only

---

[7] http://mises.org/daily/5158/Mises-on-Mind-and-Method

[8] See http://mises.org/th/intro.asp)

[9] See http://changingminds.org/explanations/research/philosophies/positivism.htm

investigate the natural laws of cause and effect. This means that to scientifically study human thinking, choices and action must be *reduced* to the study of the firings of neurons in the human brain, or some other purely materialistic explanation. This viewpoint is referred to as *reductionist* because all human actions are deemed to be reducible to materialistic cause and effect going backwards in a deterministic chain to the beginning of time. It is explicit in the writings of Dr. Berns and Dr. Harris.

What the positivist refuses to acknowledge (or acknowledge but deems to be trivial) is that the study of the firing of neurons in the human brain will never be able to predict and account for an explanation of human action. In fact, scientific knowledge about the content of our thinking at the molecular level of brain activity does not exist today except as speculative theory. What technology can reveal is the general location in the brain where neurons are firing, and brain activity is taking place. What it can *never* reveal is the thinking itself. It is a wishful fantasy on the part of positivist neuro-scientists to believe that a statistical analysis of blood flow in the brains of experimental subjects can tell us anything about what people are thinking or provide predictive ability with regards to the behaviour that will follow.

Positivism obliterates as meaningful any recognition of normative judgments and ends-intended behaviour.

When studying people, a proper methodology must embrace the fact that human action is caused by human choices and driven by human motives and values. We are aware of the "actions" of thought to the extent we can be through introspection, of which we are each capable. As Dr. Locke reminds us, in the human-based social sciences, introspection has to be a core method. It is the human means of understanding human-motives and actions. "You need to know what is going on in your own mind," writes Dr. Locke, "and you cannot get there by staring at neurons. You can neither form nor grasp psychological concepts without introspection…. The introspective knowledge required to validate consciousness and validation, being self-evident and being axiomatic, does not require further validation—only identification and explanation." (Locke, *The Illusion of Determinism*: 114)

There is no other valid way beyond introspection, verbal reports, and explanations to understand human action. No predictive knowledge can be gained by reducing human thought and intentions to neural events in the brain.

Chapter 12

THE METHODOLOGY OF SCIENCE: INDUCTION VERSUS DEDUCTION

If you start with the premise that humans lack volitional consciousness – that they lack the ability to control their thoughts and actions – then it follows that all differences between individuals must be driven by uncontrollable forces of physical and genetic causality. This necessarily must include all brain activity. If one begins with the assumption that the brain has no capability of conscious and volitional self-regulation through some methodological means that we refer to as thinking, then one can avoid looking to differences in these areas when studying the behavior of iconoclasts. This is an illegitimate rationalistic approach to conducting research based on asserting false or unsubstantiated premises to rationalize a desired conclusion. This reductionist approach leads Dr. Berns to talk about brains as if they have an independent existence separate from the people who house them, leaving the reader feeling that his argument lacks coherence and a basis in reality because the evidence is not tied back to reality.

This methodology of abstracting away the person and dealing only with the brain, and then reversing the process by using deduction to derive conclusions about the total person based only on concepts and knowledge about the brain, is exactly the opposite of the proper inductive method of science. A valid methodology requires that all premises be demonstrated as valid by their direct tie through sense perception back to reality, and that conclusions are tied back to premises and foundational first-order concepts without contradiction, so that the entire structure stands as an objective and integrated whole consistent with all of our knowledge. All knowledge is a unity, and no knowledge can be valid until it is integrated, without contradiction, into that unity. Non-contradictory integration is a requirement of logical proof.

This understanding of induction and deduction is not something new to the field of business. It is the method by which we come to know reality, from which we come to formulate knowledge to guide our actions and pursue intended results, apart from any particular field of endeavor. There is no other valid method.

There are some business leaders who write about business topics as if philosophy matters, trying to take proper and thoughtful approach to business purpose and methodology. One such business leader was 20th century British industrialist, parliamentarian, and MBE recipient, Wilfred Brown.[10] Brown wrote about his explorations in management practice as CEO of the Glacier Metal Company in his 1971 book *Organization*. In his desire to explore ideas to improve the role of workplace organizations in the lives of their workers, he hired industrial psychologist Elliott Jaques to understand how work was getting done at Glacier Metal, and how it could be improved. The project became known as the

---

[10] http://en.wikipedia.org/wiki/Wilfred_Brown,_Baron _Brown

Glacier Project which ran from 1949 to 1965, and which Peter Drucker called "the most extensive study of actual worker behavior in large-scale industry" (quoting Wikipedia).

In *Organization*, Wilfred Brown has a chapter on concept formation, in which he cites British mathematician Karl Pearson (who was influential in Albert Einstein's early theoretical thinking) on the topic of establishing the objective validity of concepts through their necessary link back to perceptions. Brown quotes Pearson: "In order that a conception may have scientific validity it must be self-consistent and deducible from the perceptions of the normal human being. For instance, a centaur is not a self-consistent conception; as soon as our knowledge of human and equine anatomy became sufficiently developed the centaur became an unthinkable thing—a self-negating idea." (Brown, *Organization*, Heineman Educational Books Ltd., London, 1971: 19).

What Wilfred Brown is talking about is the primacy of induction as a valid means to objectively identify concepts and validate them by directly linking them back to reality. Once concepts can be validated, they can be applied *deductively* to expand and extend human knowledge.

At the core of all human knowledge is sense perception, which is our objective starting point for formulating valid concepts of increasing abstraction. As long as these concepts can be derived from sense perception and tied back to sense perception, they can never become "floating abstractions" that are without a direct tie back to reality, such as are centaurs, dragons, or unicorns.

Why is this topic of concept formation important? As Wilfred Brown puts it, "If our concepts are not consistent with those used by others then we shall assume that we are each discussing the same situation when, in fact, we are not. If our concepts are not deducible from our perceptions (as in the example of the centaur which Pearson uses), then we may be attempting to discuss something that does not exist. If our concepts are not stated in boundary-defined form, then it is not possible to determine whether the thing exists or not." (Brown, *Organization*: 20).

For an excellent introduction to the proper place of induction and deduction as the methodology of science, see David Harriman's *The Logical Leap: Induction in Physics* (New American Library, 2010). Harriman briefly summarizes the differences this way:

> Deduction is a simple form of reasoning. It starts with a causal connection already conceptualized and formulated as a generalization. In other words, it starts with a complex conceptual product regarded as established and unproblematic. The deducer is not as such concerned with the process of conceptualizing complex data. He takes for granted from the outset that we have solved all the difficult epistemological questions involved in forming and using concepts. He takes as a given that the conceptual faculty has been used to gain profound new knowledge, and that it has been used properly. He then proceeds to milk the new knowledge for its implications.
>
> In contrast, an inductive argument is not a self-contained series of premises from which the conclusion follows as a matter of formal

consistency. The reason is that the bridge from observation to generalization is not one premise, or even a hundred premises, but the total of one's knowledge properly integrated. That is why induction is so much more difficult and controversial than deduction ....

Deduction takes for granted the process of conceptualization. Induction is the concept-tualizing process itself in action. (Harriman, *The Logical Leap*: 34-35)

Knowledge is not *deduced* from intuitions or speculations or a presumed set of "first causes" to rationalize or justify our beliefs about the nature of reality; it is always and everywhere *induced* from direct first-hand experience of reality.

Mr. Harriman demonstrates in detail as an example of inductive reasoning in science how iconoclast Isaac Newton developed the experimental method in physics to ensure an *inductive* approach to the discovery and proof of knowledge about the world. By proving and identifying the relationship between causes and their effects in mathematical terms, Newton was able to validate new knowledge about the world that led to further predictions, discoveries, and inventions.

On the other hand, "Newton's opponents," writes Mr. Harriman,

could not grasp that knowledge is gained by starting with observations and proceeding step by step to the discovery of causes, and eventually to the discovery of fundamental causes. They wished to start with the first causes and deduce the entire science of physics from them. Newton knew that this rationalist method led to the indulgence of fantasy, not to scientific knowledge.... Scientists who follow the rationalist method attempt to bypass the process of discovery. Using nothing more than imagination and deduction, they fabricate whole sciences discovering no knowledge, while leaving no questions unanswered. Newton's inductive method leads to the opposite result: an enormously expanded context of knowledge, with each discovery giving rise to further questions. (Harriman, *The Logical Leap*: 142).

A key attribute of the inductive method is that it is self-corrective. "This feature of the method follows from the demand that every idea must be induced from observational evidence and integrated without contradiction into the whole of available knowledge. A false idea cannot live up to this standard." (Harriman, *The Logical Leap*: 210).

A proper methodology based on induction, where truth is determined by demonstrable adherence to our current knowledge of reality, is open to changes based on further investigation and discoveries of the causal relationships that exist in the world. "A proper method keeps one in cognitive contact with reality, and therefore any clash between a false idea and reality is eventually revealed." (Harriman, *The Logical Leap*: 210).

The potential for self-correction inherent in the inductive method demonstrates that misapplication or errors provide only minor setbacks that are overcome in the normal course of further research and investigation.

But when the inductive method is rejected or opposed, progress is halted. The failure to validate higher-level abstract concepts by tying them back down to direct observation of reality from which they must be linked to be valid leaves them floating free from a valid reality-based foundation.

The existence or lack thereof of a direct connection or tie to reality is what differentiates valid concepts from invalid concepts. Invalid concepts lack correspondence with reality and therefore of necessity do not pertain to anything in reality and cannot have any factual explanatory value with regards to actual natural events. Invalid concepts contradict reality and therefore cannot be integrated with other knowledge. The attempt to integrate invalid concepts with valid knowledge (or worse, to hold onto invalid concepts at the expense of true knowledge) is to forgo any claim to objectivity and truth. To paraphrase Mr. Harriman, by rejecting observational evidence as the only objective criteria for evaluating truth or falsehood, all one is left with is the subjective criterion of one's feelings. Such was the methodology applied to science by Rene Descartes. Mr. Harriman writes: "Despite posturing as a staunch advocate of reason, he accepts the ideas he feels are true, i.e., those ideas he wants to believe. He declares that these ideas have the special intrinsic qualities that make their truth manifest" (Harriman, *The Logical Leap*: 213).

Descartes rejected sense perception as the starting point for knowledge. Instead he proceeded to develop his treatise on physics by starting with "clear and distinct" ideas he held in his mind as the truth. As a result, Mr. Harriman informs us, in contrast to the inductive and painstaking experimentation later conducted by Newton,

Descartes "made no observations, did no experiments, and engaged in no reasoning from effects to underlying causes. Instead he looked inward and offered a 'clear and distinct' make-believe world that was more imaginative than any fairy tale" (Harriman, *The Logical Leap*: 213).

Mr. Harriman concludes that the adherence to the method of deduction, rather than induction, allowed Descartes to offer his theories of physics as science even though in every case discussed he gives the wrong answer, with one minor exception. Descartes' method of deduction freed him from worrying about contradictions with regards to his personal observations of reality. With regards to the laws of motion, Descartes wrote that his deductions were so certain that even if experience seemed to show the opposite, we should still rely on our faith in reason over the evidence of our senses (see Harriman, *The Logical Leap*: 214). In dealing with earthly phenomena, Descartes wrote that "there is nothing visible or perceptible in this world that I have not explained."

"As one historian of science [A. Rupert Hall] has noted:", writes Mr. Harriman, "'Descartes left nothing untouched.... The *Principles* was a triumph of fantastic imagination which happens, unfortunately, never once to have hit upon a correct explanation.'" Mr. Harriman continues:

> Of course, there is a reason why he never 'hit upon' the truth: As we have seen, science is not a guessing game. Descartes' generalizations did not correspond to reality because he did not derive them inductively from observations of reality.

In contrast to induction, the method of rationalism is not self-corrective. If a theory is validated by intrinsic qualities such as clarity or mathematical beauty, then it cannot be overthrown by observational evidence. The theory is merely an integration of floating abstractions, detached from perceptual data and therefore invulnerable to such data. When he wishes, the rationalist is always free to further decorate his theory with 'beautiful' i.e., arbitrary – features in order to deduce any particular facts.

Cartesian physics was overthrown only when Newton rejected rationalism and demonstrated the power of the inductive method, which then gained widespread acceptance during the Enlightenment. Unfortunately, the commitment to this method did not last. (Harriman, *The Logical Leap*: 215)

As we will see, it is also important to recognize that a valid methodology is required when studying goal directed behavior as distinct from the causal laws of nature because the methodology must take into consideration the ineffable element of choice, agency, and contextual action, that exists in animate matter and which doesn't exist in inanimate matter. But while the methodology for studying human action is different, it still must be arrived at and validated inductively.

As an example in methodological contrasts in the social sciences, one can look at the inductive methodology taken by Dr. Edwin Locke in his study of the traits of great business creators (Locke, *The Prime Movers: Traits of the Great Wealth Creators*, Amacom, 2000), or Jim Collins in his study of successful business practices as reported in his book *Good To Great*, as compared to the non-inductive, rationalistic, approach taken by Dr. Berns.

The productive geniuses of wealth creation in business and industry that had immense impact on the world are identified by Dr. Locke as "prime movers," and would likely be recognized as Iconoclasts by Dr. Berns. Dr. Locke identifies such luminaries as J.P. Morgan, John Paul Getty, Henry Ford, Bill Gates, Richard Branson, Thomas J. Watson Jr., and Walt Disney, just to name a few.

Dr. Locke's methodology involves studying the lives of these individuals and identifying perceivable traits that they hold in common. "I identified the traits through induction," writes Dr. Locke in the Preface. "The traits are based on the study of more than seventy wealth creators" (Locke: x). From Dr. Locke's perspective, these aren't men and women with brains that are different in kind from the rest of humanity. Rather, they are "men of intelligence, vision, morality, and passion (x-xi)," who think as an act of choice and take action based on their thinking, and who move society forward "by the force of their own creative imagination, their own energy, and their own productive capacity" (Locke, *The Prime Movers*: 7).

Dr. Locke concludes that these Prime Movers have achieved their success because of traits they nurtured and acted on, guided by thought to engage in productive work. Dr. Locke doesn't consider whether the brains of Prime Movers and Wealth Creators are biologically different. How could he know, and what could that show? He concludes that what a person does with his brain makes all the difference in this world, not whether one is born with the *kind of brain* that will make a difference in this world.

Underlying every aspect of Dr. Locke's analysis is the premise that man has free will, without which he would be unable to conceive and formulate ideas and devise and act on complex plans of action often over a timespan of decades, to bring those visions and plans into reality. Without the guidance of ideas, says Dr. Locke, "action is just mindless motion without direction, purpose, or value" (Locke, *The Prime Movers*: 19).

Mindless motion is at best meaningless action. This is exactly the mindless and meaningless action which is, according to Dr. Berns, as demonstrated by neuro-science, the apex of what most humans are capable of exhibiting.

Chapter 13

ELLIOTT JAQUES: AN INDUCTIVE ALTERNATIVE SCIENTIFIC PERSPECTIVE

The late psychiatrist, social scientist, organizational theorist, author, and business consultant, Elliott Jaques, has provided some recent important and original insights that throw further light on the issues we have been discussing. Dr. Jaques is best known for his ground-breaking work and systems thinking about how to structure and organize businesses to ensure maximum participation, psychological fulfillment, and engagement by employees to maximize the achievement of the business purpose. In addition to numerous books, Jaques is the author to two important articles published by Harvard Business Review: "Taking Time Seriously in Evaluating Jobs" (1979), and "In Praise of Hierarchy" (1990).

Dr. Jaques observed that there is considerable confusion around issues of mind-matter, mind-brain, and mind-body and that if we are to understand life and the behaviour of living organisms on scientific terms that we can claim as knowledge, these confusions need to be clarified.

In his effort to develop a general theory of the behaviour of living organisms, Dr. Jaques felt the need to address these confusions, and did so in his final book, *The Life and Behavior of Living Organisms: A General Theory* (Praeger, 2002, referred to as *LABOLO*). Dr. Jaques presents a strong and integrated inductive argument rooted in observable facts which requires a valid refutation by those who find fault in it, not just assertions of disagreement or casual dismissal. I will summarize the essentials of Dr. Jaques argument as they pertain to the context of free will and determinism in considerable detail because I think that he brings immense value and insight to the issues we have been discussing.

In the next few sections I quote extensively from Dr. Jaques in order to fully present the essentials of Dr. Jaques' thesis as it relates to the issues of brain, mind, body, free will, and the methodology of reductionism, that is a major threat to the ongoing healthy functioning of businesses, and therefore, by extension, a threat to the health and well-being of all members of modern societies where work is primarily carried out in hierarchical managerial systems.

Chapter 14

WORK AND THE DYNAMICS OF CHOICE

Dr. Jaques begins by recognizing that all living organisms are endowed by nature with actual and potential capability that allows them to survive. "All of these forms of life," writes Dr. Jaques, "are to be distinguished in a fundamental way from the world of inanimate things and inanimate processes, mechanical, electrical, and quantum-mechanical (including, above all, computers in their present form and in the future)" (Jaques, *LABOLO*: 5-6).

Dr. Jaques observes that the study of organisms requires a dynamic approach that takes into account goal-directed movement and "behavioral motion."

In an important passage that lays down the foundation for his thinking about these matters, Dr. Jaques writes:

the meaning of movement in all living organisms is not that of physical movement as in the case of physical bodies, but that of an organism's working in the world of action, toward the achievement of a goal that it has chosen to achieve. All organisms that are alive are engaged continuously at work in goal-seeking behavior, and that is the central characteristic that means that they are alive. It is precisely by working to achieve goals that organisms survive, adapt, interact, and reproduce.

From this point of view, no processes such as perception, thinking, feeling, desiring, imagining, or even cognition are dynamic in their own right. They are dynamic only to the extent that they are carried out in relation to the organism's attempts to reach a goal. Dynamics in behavior are concerned, always and exclusively, with working and movement toward a goal. (Jaques, *LABOLO*: 7-8, italics in original.)

For Dr. Jaques, the dynamics in living behaviour is best exemplified in work:

Work is at the heart of goal-directed behavior, and all behavior is goal directed. All living organisms have to work to survive, to adapt, to reproduce, to communicate. Work lies at the heart of all living processes. Thus, for example, in human terms, we do not engage in thinking for its own sake, but as part of working to get something done; we reason as part of working to get somewhere; we look and search, as part of working to carry out some intention.... Living work has to do with the use of judgment in making choices and decisions. Unending making of choices" (Jaques, *LABOLO*: 4-5).

To understand life and to study it, says Dr. Jaques, one must recognize and acknowledge that organisms, and especially humans, "are engaged in choosing goals, choosing how to work towards achieving them, and choosing to overcome obstacles along the way" (Jaques, LABOLO, p. 5). Thus, says Dr. Jaques, it is obvious that an understanding of living behaviour requires a dynamic rather than static approach, and that a methodology different from that in physics is required: "there is no such thing as statics in living behavior. Living behavior is by simple definition, dynamic. Static behavior is not behavior" (Jaques, *LABOLO*: 8).

To properly study and make advances in understanding the nature of human capability requires an approach that can study man in motion, i.e., *goal-seeking behaviour over time*. For this reason Dr. Jaques puts little credence in the search for knowledge through questionnaires, opinion studies, personality inventories, experiments in thinking, and studies of cognition – and I would suppose also neuroimaging – unless they are actively connected with subjects engaged in goal-directed work with the use of judgment and the making of decisions.

No Choice But To Choose

Chapter 15

THE THREE SUB-FUNCTIONS OF ORGANISMS

Dr. Jaques begins with the three different sets of functions or systems that exist in all organisms, including humans. These systems are required to maintain the constant action living organisms require to stay alive. He identifies these as: *physiological*, *phylogenetic*, and *ontogenetic* functions. The first two pertain to the whole species. Only the last are associated with particular individuals and hence to individual choice and decision-making (Jaques, *LABOLO*: 10). Here is a brief description of each.

The *physiological* subsystems include neuronal, immune, endocrine, digestive, circulatory, muscular, and reproductive, and "constitute one way of analyzing living organisms in terms of their parts." All must work together in an integrated fashion to sustain an organism's life. While the physiological subsystems influence the behaviour of the organism as a whole, Dr. Jaques notes that they do not have a "direct one-to-one relationship with the working choices made by the organism. Even the neural subsystem, including the brain and particular parts of the brain, while necessary for certain behaviors, are nevertheless not sufficient to explain particular judgments and choice behaviors. They provide a field, which may be broad or narrow, within which the choices can be made" (Jaques, *LABOLO*: 10).

The *phylogenetic* functions are those genetically founded within the species and affected by the evolutionary process. They pertain to innate capabilities or instinctual actions, are related to particular gene systems, and are potentially understandable in terms of molecular biology (Jaques, *LABOLO*: 10). As with the physiological subsystems, "the gene-driven influences set the direction of behavior, the field context. They do not and cannot explain the detailed judgments, choices, and decisions under the particular circumstances obtaining at the moment of action" (Jaques, *LABOLO*: 11).

The third category, the *ontogenetic* functions, pertain to particular individual organisms, and have to do with the particular ways individual organisms "go about their goal-seeking business, choosing goals, choosing pathways to the goals, and choosing ways to overcome obstacles on the way to these goals" (Jaques, *LABOLO*: 11). The possible actions and the way an organism goes about them will be influenced by genetic forces, physiological conditions of the organism at the time, and the environmental surrounding conditions. "These conditions, however," writes Dr. Jaques, "determine the field of available choices, and not the particular final choices and decisions themselves" (Jaques, *LABOLO*: 11).

Dr. Jaques identifies that the choices involved in human decision-making must operate within the limits set by the physiological and genetic boundaries, plus specific socially identified rules, regulations, legislation, and values. He refers to these choices as the proactive "fine tuning" of decision making and goal seeking.

This fine-tuning is immensely significant to our discussion because the question of its veracity forms the crux of the answer to the question of man's free will and the meaning and impact of the work and conclusions being drawn by neuroscientists, and its influence on our understanding of ourselves and our world. Dr. Jaques writes:

> The fine tuning is the proactive part of decision making and goal seeking. It requires the setting of goals, whether intuitively or in well-articulated form. And that goal setting requires the construction of the future, that is, the setting of something to be obtained, or somewhere to get to, at some time, perhaps in seconds, or minutes, or hours, or in the case of adult humans, even in days, or months, or years.

> These fine-tuned choices and decisions are not programmed. They are idiosyncratic. They are not fully linked or linkable to any parts of the organism, not even to the brain in organisms that happen to have brains. They are products of the dynamic functioning of the total organism, and that is that. The results of the choices that are made are readily observable, but how the choices are made is not accessible. This ineffability, this hidden nature of the choice process, we refer to as free will. All living organisms have it, but it is a complete function of the total organism, not reducible to any parts. (Jaques, *LABOLO*: 11)

In summarizing, Dr. Jaques writes that living organisms

> have two separate sets of biological parts, physiological and phylogenetical, each related to the behavior of the organism, and a set of choice functions that need to be analyzed into dynamic steps rather than into interconnected biological parts. These complexities arise

because of the obvious fact that living organisms are whole systems whose outstanding features are twofold: first, they are heavily engaged in keeping themselves alive and in good condition; second, they carry their own driver as a feature of the system, but the driver in an odd way is not part of the system, but the whole system itself. (Jaques, *LABOLO*: 11-12)

It is important to recognize that the three subsystems are subsystems of the whole entity, and "crucial" not to mix them or treat them as one "in direct interaction with the other" (Jaques, *LABOLO*: 12). Doing so, says Dr. Jaques, is likely to draw attention "away from the dynamics of idiosyncratic ontogenetic behavior itself." (Jaques, *LABOLO*: 13).

Chapter 16

THE "FOOLHARDY" ERRORS OF REDUCTIONISM AND THE PROBLEM OF MIND

We have indicated already how Dr. Berns adopts a reductionist approach to the study of human behavior and how materialism entails the rejection of the irrefutable axioms of existence and consciousness.. Dr. Jaques describes reductionism as "the process of understanding and explaining complex processes by more basic processes and finally by molecular biology or by molecular physics" (Jaques, *LABOLO*: 73). "The reductionist analysis," he writes, "can be applied, and with very practical gains, to the physiological and to the phylogenetic functions. But to try to apply such analysis to the ontogenetical judgment, choice and free will functions, is what I would call false reductionism and is simply foolhardy." The fact is, says Dr. Jaques, "individual behavior is a function of whole individual organisms as total systems" (Jaques, *LABOLO*: 74).

The "foolhardy" nature of reductionism lies in the attempt to account for the total human being by denying an essential feature of its nature – the ability to apply its consciousness in a volitional manner towards the pursuit of goal directed action over time. It is also foolhardy says Dr. Jaques, because it attempts to separate humans as a whole living entity and "total system" into two distinct but illusionary parts: mind and body.

The idea of a separate mind and body and talk of humans as having both has a long 2,500-year history, so it is not surprising that the confusion in the common language we use regarding brains, minds, and bodies as separate and distinct entities creates a lack of clarity of concepts. Dr. Jaques is a stickler for clarity of concepts because they are a requirement of knowledge. As he sees it, "It is no longer practical or realistic to float along without rigorously and univocally constructed concepts. Undefined concepts end up in slovenly language underpinning slovenly thought. The first and most fundamental step in the construction of any science is to develop a univocally defined taxonomy" (Jaques, *LABOLO*: 13). It is time to recognize the error in such concepts and set them aside for good, says Dr. Jaques. Improperly defined concepts accepted as valid knowledge are a barrier to the discovery of truth and lead to unsuccessful linkages between human intentions and chosen action, and ultimately, to unsuccessful results.

Dr. Jaques calls the concept of *mind* "one of the unicorns of philosophy and psychology, and nowadays of neuropsychology" (Jaques, *LABOLO*: 75). He refers to the problem as a unicorn because you can easily say the word 'unicorn' and easily draw one, but that doesn't mean you can go out and find one to study. The allegory holds when it comes to talk of body and mind:

> Once you have split the whole living organism into two parts, one part called the body and the other part called the mind, you are caught on the horn (unicorn horn) of a harsh dilemma. You can look everywhere, but nowhere will you find a *separate part* called a mind. A bit more difficult to realize, you cannot even find a

separate part called a body. Cars may have separate parts called bodies; living organisms do not. A body is not a part of a living organism; it is the whole of a dead carcass.

Not only can you not find the mind, but if you could, you would have a mindless body "driven" by a bodiless mind. The problem is that a mindless body is a corpse, and a freestanding bodiless mind is a fantasy. Having separated them, we are faced with the problem of how to figure out not only how a fantasy can tell a body what to do, but also how a body can produce sensations and thoughts in a fantasy. (Jaques, *LABOLO*: 75, italics in original.)

Once you separate the whole person into two separate parts – body and mind – the problem of how to put them back together is irresolvable. What must be recognized, notes Dr. Jaques, is the fundamental error of breaking the whole system into an outside component (body) and an inside component (mind) in the first place. As long as we remain fixated on the incorrect idea that minds and bodies are separate things that can coexist independently as we search for the source of living activity – of how the brain can accomplish reasoning and have experiences – we lose sight of the total organism, the total person. "Remember," Dr. Jaques reminds us, "the driver of living organisms is not a separate homunculus seated on a cortical throne somewhere in the head, but the total organism itself, or yourself (but not, note, your 'self')." (Jaques, *LABOLO*: 76).

"The short answer to these questions [of mind and body]," concludes Dr. Jaques,

is that neither brains nor physical nor mechanical systems can reason, or have experiences, or have thoughts. And yet as long as we continue to maintain a mind-body dichotomy, we translate body into brain, and are trapped in an orientation that inexorably calls for attempts to explain complex organical judgment and choice processes in physical, mechanical, neurological, or other physiological terms. In so doing, we are continuing along the path set by Descartes....

Somehow to be able to find relationships between observable activity in certain parts of the brain while the organism is carrying out certain functions is reassuring to many people. There is no evidence, however, that what is being observed is the source of the ontogenetic free will behaviors of the organism, but only a necessary underpinning for these processes. Despite this fact, it somehow feels more scientific to have a material or mechanical explanation, just as being able to understand certain phenomena in the field of chemistry in terms of basic physical laws was a significant development in the natural sciences. (Jaques, *LABOLO*: 76)

It is a defining characteristic of reductionists to treat the brain as the person, ascribing to it all the things that a person would do, including thinking, perceiving, feeling, deciding, etc., and thereby ignore that what is being considered is really a person. Dr. Jaques postulates that "This kind of exercise in unwarranted reductionism from ontogenetic whole to physiological part seems to make many scientists more intellectually comfortable than they would otherwise be. There is something more reassuring and manageable about an unequivocal brain than there is about a seemingly much less certain person." (Jaques, *LABOLO*: 79)

According to Dr. Jaques, the physiological and phylogenetic processes alone are not sufficient to explain the needs, intentions, goals, language and communications, choices and judgments of individuals in the unique situations in which they must act. "These ontogenetical life processes cannot be reduced to physiology via phylogenetics, nor via physiology to physics" (Jaques, *LABOLO*: 81).

Chapter 17

FREE WILL CAN NOT BE EXPLAINED AWAY

To summarize Dr. Jaques argument, critical errors are made in the study of how man discovers, understands, develops, and uses knowledge when there is a failure to recognize the existence and importance of all three subsystems as components of a whole system. Those who tend to dismiss the reality of the action of people inherent in the ontogenetic function of goal directed action tend to ignore or deny the reality of individual judgment and choice in formulating goals to achieve work objectives. Instead they focus on the two systems related to maintenance behaviours that are compatible with biological causality and reductionist arguments i.e., physiological and phylogenetic.

In other words, as Dr. Jaques puts it, "the two life maintenance sets of processes, physiological and phylogenetical, are the unfree aspects of living behavior. The judgment/choice organical work processes are what might be called free will" (Jaques, *LABOLO*: 81). It is precisely by this faulty method of ignoring or diminishing the reality of human choice and judgment, often combined with an unwarranted embracing of the mind/body dichotomy as an unquestioned axiomatic premise, that reductionists and determinists come to embrace the pretense of explaining away volitional consciousness and free will in humans.

Dr. Jaques rightly recognizes that all attempts to reduce the judgment/choice processes of individuals to physiological functions must fail, with the result being that "[w]e might have to accept living choicing and decision making for what they are and content ourselves with observing their outcomes and understanding them in their own right" (Jaques, *LABOLO*: 83).

Much of the absurdity of the anti-free will position can be seen when we shift from an artificially narrow abstract theoretical discussion to more practical implications that require a wider integration of our knowledge. That free will cannot be explained away "make[s]...reductionists look a bit silly if and when they go too far," says Dr. Jaques, such as when they suggest in earnest opinions that solutions to mankind's moral, social, political and economic problems can be found by studying the brain. (Jaques, *LABOLO*: 82.)

For a representative example of the kind of misguided research Dr. Jaques was referring to, see the article "Using Neuroscience to Learn How to Build a Better Leader."[11] The article describes how a team of researchers at the W.P. Carey School of Business are engaged in "organizational neuro-scientific research" in which they are studying the brain using EEG technology to identify leadership qualities in individuals. Their aim is to develop exercises "that should allow individuals to alter their brain activity to become more effective leaders."

I suspect that Dr. Jaques would see this as an example of misguided and "silly" research because there are no leadership qualities to be found *in* the

---

[11] https://news.wpcarey.asu.edu/20110504-using-neuroscience-learn-how-build-better-leader, May 12, 2011

brain. Dr. Jaques defined leadership very precisely as "that process in which one person sets the purpose or direction for one or more other persons, and gets them to move along together with him or her and with each other in that direction with competence and full commitment" (E. Jaques and S. Clement, *Executive Leadership*, Blackwell, 1994: 4). Leadership is a critical component of management, requiring the practical application of concepts, principles and values in the use of judgment and the making of choices in pursuit of defined work goals over time. Dr. Jaques would argue, as indicated in what I have presented of his argument above, that those studying leadership in this manner don't really understand what leadership is or how to study it. Recall Dr. Jaques' observation that the study of humans requires a dynamic approach that studies man in motion engaged in goal-seeking behaviour over time. To think that the best way to identify leadership qualities is to study brains via EEGs and MRIs rather than to talk to real leaders and study actual leadership behavior seems like a step backwards. It's like trying to learn to play the piano by studying EEGs of accomplished pianists. It's the wrong means to achieve the ends aimed for. It can't be done.

Human beings are not made up of bodies and minds. Dr. Jaques writes that "to the extent that we take bodies and minds to express an initial analysis of humans into two basic parts, then real problems arise. For mindless bodies and bodiless minds just do not exist. They are mere fantasies, unicorns, figments of the philosophical imaginations." (Jaques, *LABOLO*: 84).

As Dr. Jaques notes, the attempt to substitute "judgmental choice processes" that constitute free will with reductionist references to "bodies, minds, brains, neurons, or whatever...is unsound, dysfunctional, distracting, misleading, and above all totally and manifestly unnecessary." (Jaques, *LABOLO*: 84).

Once again it is useful to quote Dr. Jaques at length as he provides a comprehensive conclusion and devastating critique of the error of the mind/body dichotomy we see at the root of reductionism and prominent in the thinking of many neuro-scientists such as Dr. Berns and their disciples:

> If we ask what is it that our minds do, or our brains, or our bodies, or our neuronal systems do, to determine what we say, what we choose to note or choose to do, as persons, the answer is that they provide a necessary underpinning for such processes of choicing and working, but that they are decidedly insufficient to explain them. These problems can be overcome once we recognize that it is we the whole persons who work, choose, speak, and observe. It is the person who decides to go to dinner at the French restaurant around the corner, not the person's mind (even though he or she might colloquially opine "I'm minded to go to dinner"), nor the person's brain, nor a cognitive process contained within a cognitive network or within a brain.
>
> In short, the mind-body and related dichotomies are misleading because they are based on inaccurate and confused assumptions about the nature of the parts of the whole living systems.... In the case of the mind-body dichotomy itself, this inaccuracy is extreme: it is to divide the whole organisms or at least human

beings into two fantastical *imaginary parts*, both equally unreal. Such mythical and mystical analyses are unlikely to get us very far toward understanding living behavior.

How then are we to resolve the mind-body formulation that has been so tenacious and pervasive? The answer, I suggest, is really very simple. Abandon it! Eliminate it! Scrub it! Fortunately, bodies and minds are unnecessary, for, as I repeat, you will find that there is absolutely nothing that our mythical mind can do that we as live whole persons cannot do better. (Jaques, *LABOLO*: 84).

Chapter 18

DOES NEUROECONOMICS EXIST? CONJECTURE OR EVIDENCE?

What started off sounding like it may be a reasonable theory (though shrouded in the language of brain science) and presented by a leading professor at a leading university (Emory) by the leading business book publisher (Harvard Business Press), appears upon deeper reflection to be a confused and full-out frontal attack on man's faculty of reason and thus on the pivotal foundations of successful entrepreneurship and economic wealth creation. It is an attack on the concept of human consciousness, human agency, free will and the need for people to continually apply judgment in making choices to sustain their lives and achieve their aspirational goals and everyday ends. *Iconoclast* appears to be an attempt to justify a positivist theoretical construct rather than a presentation of convincing evidence derived inductively and logically from demonstrated facts and evidence.

Dr. Berns' thesis on Iconoclasts is a rationalistic and deterministic theory of human behavior based on an arbitrary postulation of how the brain is *supposed* to function. It consists of a series of interesting anecdotes strung together with false or dubious philosophic and scientific ideas in an attempt to reverse-engineer a speculative "theory" to explain that iconoclasts are people who can do things that others say can't be done because there is something different about their brains. "It seems obvious," Dr. Berns writes, "that there should be something different in the brains of [iconoclasts], but because these individuals are rare, it is difficult to pin down what these differences might be" (Berns, *Iconoclast*: 119).

In other words, in the end, Dr. Berns admits that after all his puffery, he really has no scientific facts to support his conclusion that iconoclasts have different brains. Rather, he is engaging in radical speculation fraudulently being sold under the pretense of the latest scientific evidence from neuroscience, that somehow iconoclasts must be able to do something others can't that is enabled by their unique possession of the phenomenon of free will.

It only "seems obvious" that the brains of some people are different in kind from the brains of all other people, and that we can know these differences by observing their "iconoclastic behavior," if we already accept the dubious premise that people are pre-programmed biological machines, like robot-puppets incapable of goal-directed action and self-control, or as Dr. Jaques identifies it, incapable of ontogenetic capabilities. Dr. Berns accepts this premise, writing that some people have "the iconoclast brain" (*Iconoclast*: 120) and the rest do not. Those who have it can be identified by "others" by some unspecified mechanistic means, and as a result of such identification, can become iconoclasts. Those that do not have it are not and can never be iconoclasts. Dr. Berns is informing the aspiring non-iconoclastic business audience towards which his book is directed that they can't think differently because they literally *can't think*. This is not asserted as a normative judgment on Dr. Berns' part but is put forward as an empirical scientific fact standing at the base of his theory about human behavior and underlying his scientific endeavours.

However, if one rejects the validity of Dr. Berns' argument that neuroscience has proved people lack free will, then Dr. Berns' conclusion that iconoclasts have a biologically different 'iconoclast' brain for which "it is difficult to pin down what these differences might be" doesn't seem obvious at all. After reading his book, his conclusion seems obviously wrong. Brain scans may reveal areas of blood flow signifying electro-magnetic brain events, but they can't reveal the thinking that is occurring in the brain. It is the nature of all healthy human brains to gather sense data in the form of perceptions, form concepts, hold values, exert judgment in assessing desires, and form pathways to goals pursued through action directed towards the achievement of life-serving future outcomes. It is the willful exertion of individuals to think, to learn, and to direct action in the pursuit of values that gives meaning to human action. No doubt that there are genetic differences that define the potential capabilities of each individual. But it's not the latent and unknown potential that resides within our genetics that defines our achievements. Our achievements are the result of what individual people choose to do with what they have in the given situation in which they find themselves, and their internal desire to do it.[12]

---

[12] For example, see "Is There A Genius In All Of Us?" at www.bbc.co.uk/news/magazine-12140064

Chapter 19

FURTHER IMPLICATIONS OF THE NEUROECONOMIC PREMISE?

If Dr. Berns' argument is an accurate reflection of the new field of neuroeconomics, then shouldn't the basic methodology he puts forth have wider application beyond the study of iconoclasts? There is nothing that suggests that iconoclasts are a special group more worthy of neurological study than others. That being the case, we should be able to apply the same logic and evidence put forth by Dr. Berns to other identifiable groups.

Consider, for example, those who become criminals. If iconoclasts have a different iconoclastic brain, then can criminals be said to have the *criminal* brain? Do those who perform music in public have the *performer's* brain? And do those who own dogs have the *canine endeared* brain? Do those who join the military to protect the freedom of their country's citizens have the *patriot* brain? I suspect that if one were to adopt Dr. Berns' methodology these assertions would prove to be true. Why? Because if you did neuroimaging of the brains of criminals while they are engaged in criminal acts, or musicians while they are performing music, or dog owners while they are playing with their dogs, a statistical analysis of the results would show that they have higher levels of activity in the parts of their brain that support reckless risk taking or music performance or empathetic play. How could it be otherwise?

No Choice But To Choose

Chapter 20

CONCLUSION

The validity and seriousness with which we should accord to the theory put forth by Dr. Berns and his insights into "thinking differently" as representing valid contributions to management science and the entrepreneurial leader's understanding of the world and how to improve human well-being is commensurate with the scientific seriousness we should grant to Miss Anne Elk's theory about the brontosaurus (John Cleese and Monty Python): that they are thin on one end, much thicker in the middle, and thin again on the opposite end. It is perhaps ironic that the original brontosaurus was knowingly mounted with the wrong head by its discoverer, professor of paleontology at Yale University, Othniel Charles Marsh, to fabricate a complete specimen rather than deal honestly with the actual evidence at hand.[13]

What I expected to be a layman's scientific elucidation and evidential treatise on the part of Dr. Berns pertaining to traits that differentiate iconoclasts from the masses turns out not to be a treatise about or derived from the study of any real iconoclasts at all. Rather, it ends up being a mere speculative theory of the weakest kind, posing as scientific insight and endorsed by the leading academic business publisher, as being worthy of the time and attention of the world's business leaders.

---

[13] http://www.unmuseum.org/dinobront.htm

If Dr. Berns is a credible spokesperson for neuro-economics, his book is an admission by one of its leading practitioners that this new field can only produce more social harm than good by advocating that there is "scientific" support for false and questionable ideas of immense practical importance. When and if business-people *unthinkingly* adopt false ideas or are led to them by leading business institutions that they regard as highly authoritative and trustworthy for useful and practical leading-edge ideas, they put themselves on a course that clashes with reality. As businesspeople who are objectively measured by bottom line profits know better than most, in any clash between false ideas or wishful assumptions on the one hand, and reality on the other, reality always wins. Real wealth and real lives and livelihoods are on the line.

Business executives and managers are required to plan, develop and manage complex work through the massive cooperation of people and coordination of finances and operational logistics. This work requires immense competency and precision in imagination, analysis, synthesis, resource planning, social co-operation, leadership, and decision-making to solve problems in highly ambiguous and unique circumstances, sustained over long periods of time to create life-enhancing and socially beneficial goods and services. It is the responsibility of these leaders to be ever vigilant and ensure the objectivity of methods of discovery and application, and to weed out false and destructive theories and fads. Business leaders seek wealth creation, not wealth destruction.

Those who are or desire to be prime movers must be wary of any and all professed "scientific" claims when scientists put forth evidence and arguments that are contradictory and can't be integrated with the wider knowledge of the world that we know to be true. We must always be vigilant to proportion our belief to the evidence.

In this case, it is proper to reject the claims of leading neuroscience practitioners and theoreticians to the extent that they propose or endorse that science does not require inductive evidence for their "scientific" claims, and that it is sufficiently valid within a scientific framework to deduce conclusions from arbitrary premises, in this case that there *should* be something different in the brains of iconoclasts even if we don't know what those differences are. If this is what passes for science today in our most prestigious universities, and if these pseudo-scientific findings are being endorsed and taught to the next generation of business leaders and teachers in our most prestigious universities, then we are in the throes of cultural depravity. From his arbitrary assertion of what *should* be, a grand leap beyond logic is made by Dr. Berns to what he concludes therefore *must* be: that iconoclasts have different brains.

That businesses are structured and organized to achieve complex outcomes of great human ingenuity that are meaningful to people in their dual rules as employees and consumers should be sufficient evidence for entrepreneurs, managers, and iconoclasts to independently assess and judge the validity of Dr. Berns' theory. If neuroscience and neuroeconomics are based on the supposed scientific proof that human choice is an illusion, then these academic disciplines have nothing to offer anybody who possesses the desire and is motivated towards self-improvement; they are intellectual and scientific dead ends that are incapable of producing any good results, and to the extent that they clash with reality, can only produce a considerable amount of harm.

As for those real-life geniuses who are identified in *Iconoclast*, they should feel insulted, not honoured, by Dr. Berns' analysis. The implication from Dr. Berns' neuroscience and neuroeconomics perspective is that these men and women, who should be celebrated as heroes for dedicating their lives to learning, thinking, and creating to solve the mysteries of the universe and thereby improve the well-being of mankind through the creation of and contribution to heretofore unknown and incalculable value, are in reality merely human biological anomalies.

APPENDIX I

The Role of the Entrepreneur

Those who are not entrepreneurs rarely give thought to all that is involved in being one. The challenge of applying one's knowledge to the task of earning a profit in a free-market economy is daunting. To assert that entrepreneurial success can come about when free will is an illusion is preposterous. The entrepreneur is inductive evidence that determinism is false.

Faustino Ballvé in his book *Essentials of Economics: A Brief Summary of Principles and Policies* (Foundation For Economic Education, Inc., New York, 1995)[14] goes to considerable lengths to describe the role and challenges faced by the entrepreneur.

At every turn there are considerations of knowledge to be taken into account and choices to be made. As you read this extended excerpt, consider whether this a relatively accurate description of what entrepreneurs do, and whether there is any possibility of entrepreneurs developing businesses and bringing products to market for consumers, without the veracity of free will. Is every "choice" along the way fatalistically determined? Is every entrepreneur who is engaged in this behaviour and struggling to solve problems and working tirelessly to earn profits operating under an illusion that the choices being made are real choices?

---

[14] Available at https://mises.org/library/essentials-economics

Strictly speaking, the entrepreneur is anyone who goes to the market to sell or anyone who goes to the market to buy, not for his own consumption, but to resell what he has bought.

The entrepreneur aims at making a profit, and to this end he is obliged to resort to appropriate means. He thus has to exercise his power of choice twice: he has to choose the end, and he has to choose the means of attaining it. For both he has to make use of his judgment, of his own powers of reasoning. This is called *economic calculation*.

The first thing that must be done by whoever considers himself an entrepreneur and desires to enter the market to offer for sale something that will yield him a profit is to decide on the kind of thing he is going to trade in. It may be something entirely produced by him, or something he has transformed from what it was when he acquired it; or it may simply be in the same physical condition as it was when he got it, but improved in his estimation by his having kept it until the consumer needed it or by his having transported it from where it was not useful to where it is; or perhaps he has just broken it up or accumulated it in quantities acceptable to the consumer. To come to such a decision, he must study the market, that is to say, he will have to be guided by what in economics are called *the data of the market*. He has to take into account what is already in abundant supply in the market and what therefore it is not advisable to offer for sale; what is in short supply and consequently will easily find ready purchasers; what the qualities are that are predominantly in demand; whether it is expedient to offer one quality or another; and finally, what the future *prospects* of the market are, i.e., what promises to prove profitable, not now, but when he enters the market and even after that. This applies as much to goods as to services: nobody will undertake today to sell things that are out of fashion....

Having chosen the end, i.e., the kind of speculation he is going to embark on, the entrepreneur has next to concern himself with the means by which he is to carry out his project. These are called, in general, *means of production*, even though they may not involve the production of material things, but simply the rendering of services. A producer is not only one who makes shoes; he is also one who distributes them, one who transports them. All produce, in the last analysis, *commodities*; that is to say, they accommodate the consumer by satisfying his needs and desires. (Faustino Ballvé, *Essentials of Economics*, Foundation For Economic Education, New York, 1995: 19-21)

With regards to the means of production, the entrepreneur must acquire capital and labour, and put them to appropriate and productive uses, arranging "for the production of the goods or services that are to be offered for sale in the market—from the highest ranks of intellectual workers down to the humblest hired hands" (Faustino Ballvé, *Essentials of Economics*: 21).

The entrepreneur must also make decisions about the technical means of production, "choosing those that he considers to be the most adequate" among the diverse possible methods. "Each has its advantages and its disadvantages, and he has to select the one that is most appropriate for his purpose, taking into account the wants he wishes to satisfy, the processes used by his competitors, the costs involved in the use of each method, and the corresponding profit to be expected from its employment, etc., etc." (Faustino Ballvé, *Essentials of Economics*: 21, 22).

Mr. Ballvé carries on outlining additional challenges facing the entrepreneur and the nature of choices he faces and the decisions he is required to make as they relate to various economic principles, in pursuit of production for profit.

The point being made in the context of this discussion is that production and the creation of wealth requires an immense context of knowledge and continual choices across a diverse range of subjects that would be *impossible* without free will.

I look forward to an explanation on the part of deterministic neuroeconomists as to how the immense evidence of human productivity and mental activity involved in economic calculation, and exemplified in the actions of entrepreneurs, can be explained as an inevitable and accidental result of causal events dating back to the beginning of time, without reference to the ability of humans to make volitional choices. When seen in this context, I hope it is evident why the assertion of determinists that free will is an illusion, and that the weighing of evidence and application of reason and logic to make choices amongst alternative options being considered, is, on the face of it, completely incompatible with the practical requirements of business, and human life in general.

APPENDIX II

Discretion in Craft & Low-Level Roles

If determinists are right and free will is an illusion—if thinking and weighing evidence and applying judgment as the methodology for reaching conclusions and taking action are neurologically-causal fantasies—then so too must be managerial leadership in business. This would include the desire on the part of management to motivate staff to pursue a course of self-actualization, and to engage workers in purposeful coordinated action to achieve business, organizational, and personal aspirations.

Wilfred Brown, writing in his book *Organization* (Heinemann Educational Books Ltd., London, 1971), reminds us that work is not primarily physical in nature, but is the result of mental effort. Peter Drucker called this *knowledge work* and he called those who engaged in non-physical work *knowledge workers*.

A question to consider is: can work be done at all if free will is an illusion?

A general definition of work is "purposeful thought and action in pursuit of goals." Wilfred Brown provides a much more specific definition for "employment work," i.e., work being done in modern businesses that are organized and structured around managerial hierarchies. Employment work, he says, is "the application of knowledge and the exercise of discretion within limits prescribed by the immediate manager, the whole being carried out within an employment contract." (Brown, *Organization*: 384).

Of course, if free will is an illusion, there can be no "application of knowledge and exercise of discretion" as we commonly understand and use these concepts to describe acts of volition. There can also be no valid contracts. Rather, if choice is illusory, then all that our "thinking" amounts to is a *post hoc* causal mental rationalization of an imaginary decision process triggered by unconscious neural activity beyond our control and understanding. For determinists, the illusion of thinking becomes a mere artifact of nature like lightning, or magnetism, or the formation of salt crystals. The determinist position denies the possibility of actions in pursuit of chosen ends and ascribes no meaning to them.

Wilfred Brown provides an account of a craftsman to illustrate that even what may appear to be simple manual jobs often require considerable mental work and independent judgment to create the desired results. He writes:

> We can consider two aspects of work: physical work and mental effort. Many people who watch a craftsman at work assume that they are observing physical work, albeit carried out with considerable manual dexterity. At the same time, they may realize that much experience lies behind and contributes to the movements of his hands and his 'manual' performance. In fact, they are watching an activity which is largely mental, for, as soon as the physical endeavour begins to absorb even a low fraction of his total physical potential, he will call for power tools of some kind. Craftsmen are employed because they are constantly able to make wise

decisions. A craftsman's deftness, his feel and touch, are dictated by decisions made in his mind. His decisions maintain a balance between such things as quantity of output and material used, quality of output, aesthetic aspects, and perhaps many other things as well.

It ought to be easy to appreciate the constant decision-making required in a craft job. Most of us have spent time carrying out craft jobs. Cooking is a craft job and so is gardening. Nor is it difficult to appreciate that managerial, administrative and technological work largely involve decision-making. Sometimes, however, the decision-making goes unrecognized. (Brown, *Organization*: 37).

Mr. Brown goes on to discuss very simple jobs in which technological innovation has turned people into "button-pushers," and the misperception that people have about the simplicity of these jobs. While they may appear simple, they actually require considerable mental effort and an ongoing process of making choices:

Many people now believe that industrial workers are simply 'button-pushers' who make no decisions, and that the number of roles that contain responsible decision-taking work is diminishing. There is ample evidence that this is untrue. Anybody who analyzes the average 'button-pusher's' role will usually be surprised to discover how much judgment the operator has to use. His acts of judgment will involve assessing whether the machine is functioning correctly and stopping it if it is not, adjusting it, changing tools, watching and deciding on the quality of output, watching the quality of the material being fed to the machine, and deciding when to call up more supplies of material. (Brown, *Organization*: 38).

What examples such as this show is that determinists see these issues in very abstract terms that are disconnected from the real world. They too use their senses and their reason, and they make choices like the rest of us to get through life because there is no other way to live. But then when they come around to developing theories, they reason backwards from high-level conclusions through a chain of deductive logic. If everything has a cause, and if all causes are physical in nature, then so must be thinking and the process of making choices. Those choices can't be real choices because that would break the causal chain, hence there can be no choices. If we can't make choices freely, disconnected from our biological nature and neural-chemical processes of the brain, then all of our actions must be caused by such activity. Because we have the experience that we are making volitional choices and pursuing values and goals of our own choosing, the phenomenon of choice and the associated experience must be an illusion. The logic, the determinists believe, is solid. Just like Zeno's paradox.

The problem is that this logic is deductive and drops the full context in which the knowledge upon which it rests has been developed. Those who put forth such arguments fail to understand that free will is required to get to the advanced state where one can even put forth such an argument. The irony is that the argument for determinism rests on the validity of the argument for free will. The examples of these two appendices demonstrate the extent to which one must drop the context of reality and the fact that purposeful human action requires thought. I for one cannot understand how anybody can seriously put forth the proposition that all human thinking is an illusion and that humans are incapable of volitional choices. I have tried to indicate that no matter how serious such scientists and educators claim to be, there are no grounds to take them seriously.

But neither should we take them as jokesters, for these errors in philosophic and scientific thinking are no joke. There are real world consequences when scientists are incapable of clear, rational, thinking, and thereby put forth theories that clash head on with reality and undermine the underlying requirements for people to live productive lives in free-market industrial democracies.

AFTERWARDS

In the process of writing this book over a lengthy period of time, I have chosen on numerous occasions to put aside other things to concentrate on writing this book. I have researched, read, written, edited, pondered, rewritten, etc. I created, and am responsible for, the final product. By means of my act of creation and your act of reading these words, we stand together, as did Boswell and Johnson, and are able to state with full knowledge and alacrity against those scientists who put forth arguments to refute free will – "I refute it thus."

ABOUT THE AUTHOR

Since 1994 Barry Linetsky has been a Partner with The Strategic Planning Group in Toronto, Canada, working as a stealth strategic consultant to executives and their leadership teams to help them sharpen their strategic focus and understand how customer expectations of product and service performance can be used to drive enhancements across all aspects of business (strategy, structure, brand, marketing, operations, service). His lucid communication skills and analytical acumen lend additional strengths to his strong implementation and project management skills.

Barry received an Honours BA in Sociology in 1983 and an MA in Philosophy in 1985 from York University, and an MBA from University of Toronto (Rotman) in 1992.

Barry is the author of four books, including the acclaimed business biography *The Business of Walt Disney and the Nine Principles of His Success*, *Free Will: Sam Harris Has It (Wrong)*, and *Understanding and Creating Vision & Mission Statements* (with Dobri Stojsic). He was the photo editor of the best-selling *The Waterfront Trail: A Guidebook*. His thought-leadership articles have been published by Ivey Business Journal and Rotman Magazine. He blogs at www.barrylinetsky.com.

OTHER BOOKS BY BARRY L. LINETSKY

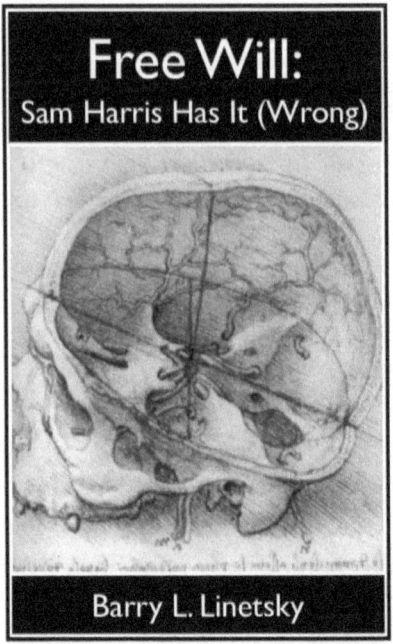

Free Will: Sam Harris Has It (Wrong)

Do humans have free will? Are we able to make choices and influence our thinking and actions? Or is all of our brain activity just the quivering of atoms based on causal antecedents ignited at the beginning of time? If the latter, then is thinking, including thinking about free will, even possible?

Does science really support that thinking, choosing, and acting in pursuit of goals and values is all just an illusion?

This short book looks at the writings of Sam Harris in his best-selling book *Free Will*. Harris asserts that science through neuroscientific research has finally established the illusion of free will and human volitional consciousness. I put forward the case that he's wrong.

What Readers are Saying about
Free Will: Sam Harris Has It (Wrong)

"Excellent short essay that professors should consider assigning to their students. ... [A]s Linetsky points out, university philosophy students can easily fall for complex arguments that they don't know how to refute.... Linetsky does the hard work of figuring out precisely why someone like Harris is wrong...[and] points to the methodological errors." **Dr. Steve Gedeon, Associate Professor, Entrepreneurship and Strategy at Ted Rogers School of Management, Ryerson University, Toronto.**

"The author aptly points out where Sam Harris accepts one form of evidence to support his conclusion and then turns around and dismisses the same form of evidence when it contradicts his desired conclusions." **Tom S.**

"In this superbly clarifying and intellectually hard-hitting essay Barry Linetsky soundly demolishes the determinist attack on free will. He also upholds a scientific methodology consistent with a view of causality that embraces volition as a special case. Given a determinist mindset, it is hard to see how a field can progress when scientists see black boxes at every point where their knowledge ends." **TommySan**

"This is a great essay. I recommend it to everyone who has read Sam Harris' Free Will. Barry Linetsky exposes many of the flaws and contradictions on Sam Harris' book, in a simple, concise, and clear manner. Read it and you will know why Sam Harris has it wrong." **Fredrico G.**

"I honestly can't think of anything in this book that actually undermined Sam Harris's book (for those who took the time to fully understand it). As a result, I'm that much more convinced of determinism." **Wpschoch**

OTHER BOOKS BY BARRY L. LINETSKY

The Business of Walt Disney and the Nine Principles of His Success

Walt Disney was the most beloved and recognized entrepreneur of the 20th Century. He was a thought-leader, change-agent, entrepreneur and iconoclast like no other. More than 50 years after his death in 1966, he remains an inspiration and symbol of imagination, excellence, and hope to hundreds of millions of people around the globe.

In this thoroughly researched and motivational business biography for a general audience, I present the detailed story of Walt Disney's dramatic and fascinating business career and draw out the nine principles of his business success as a general guide to anyone seeking personal inspiration and achievement.

What Readers are Saying about
The Business of Walt Disney and the Nine Principles of His Success

"The Business of Walt Disney is an excellent book. It is the first real attempt at telling the whole story of Walt's career purely from a business standpoint and it definitely achieves its goal. Barry has done his homework. His book is well researched and an easy read.... He makes excellent use of all the interviews that have been released via *Walt's People*...and all of the other books about Disney history that were not available to his predecessors." **Didier Ghez, Disney Historian, author, and Media & Entertainment Executive**

"This book was a page turner, packed with a great deal of information I never knew about Disney, especially during his pre-Mickey years. What Linetsky demonstrates on nearly every page is Disney's confidence and courage to go against conventional wisdom. ... Linetsky tops off the story with entrepreneurial lessons that we can learn from Disney. The book is really two books in one: the thriller story of Walt and his brother (the one who kept his eye on the finances) and the business textbook. We can all enjoy and learn much from them. **Jerry Kirkpatrick, Professor Emeritus, International Business and Marketing, California State Polytechnic University, Pomona.**

"A real page-turner! If you want an understanding of Walt Disney's life as a visionary, businessman, and a human being this book is it." **Maureen D.**

"Disney's story is inspirational—what a struggle he went through! I admire him for never compromising his art despite pressing financial concerns—and look at the success he achieved! It shows that there's no necessary conflict between being a good artist and a good businessman. My compliments to the author." **Jim W.**

OTHER BOOKS BY BARRY L. LINETSKY

Understanding and Creating Vision and Mission Statements

There isn't a more powerful engine driving organizations towards excellence and long-range success than an attractive, worthwhile, achievable, and widely shared vision of the future.

Every organization needs a purpose for its existence.

The vision and mission of an organization focuses people's attention on a common dream, ambition, or outcome. It defines a common purpose to guide behavior. It is the foundation to becoming a purpose-driven organization.

Together, a Vision and Mission statement begin to define, articulate, and communicate the purpose and values of an organization to others, including owners, executives, employees, consumers, customers, and other interested and affected people and organizations.

In this handbook, for the first time, the authors present the tools and guidance they have developed over 25-years of consulting and working with a wide-variety of blue-chip clients across a wide range of industries, including financial services, retail, hospitality, technology, sports and entertainment, government and not-for-profits.

This no-nonsense book will teach you how to formulate your thinking and to work with your colleagues to develop and refine practical and effective vision and mission statements. It includes background about the Painless Strategic Planning Process, education, exercises, examples, and instructions to follow to help you and your team understand and painlessly develop effective vision and mission statements.